Similarity Measures for Face Recognition

Authored By

Enrico Vezzetti and Federica Marcolin

Department of Management and Production Engineering
Politecnico di Torino
Torino
Italy

CONTENTS

FOREWORD

This book addresses a fundamental step in face recognition research answering, among other issues, the following questions: how to properly measure the distance between surfaces representing faces, what are the pros and contras of each algorithms and how they compare with each other, what are their computational costs. In this respect, this book represents a reference point for PhD students and researchers who want to start working not only at face recognition problems but also at other applications dealing with the recognition of three-dimensional shapes.

The need for such a book was particularly evident when we presented to our multidisciplinary team of the High Polytechnic School the topic to be studied that was aimed at the development of a diagnostic tool of prenatal syndromes from three-dimensional ultrasound scans (SYN DIAG). A book, easy to use, putting order and organizing the scientific significance of similarity measures applied to face recognition problems was missing. This aspect was crucial to support the choice of measures to be selected and tested.

Coming to the topic of the book, face recognition has several applications, including security, such as authentication and identification of suspects, and medical ones, such as corrective surgery and diagnosis. So, I think that this book is going to be a valuable tool for all scientists 'facing face'.

Luigi Preziosi

Department of Mathematical Sciences
Politecnico di Torino
Torino
Italy

PREFACE

This book is a thorough organized treatise of the current knowledge on similarity measures applied to face recognition. Firstly, an overview on measures, distance functions and metrics is given. Then, each measure is introduced, defined, and inserted in the context of face recognition through a detailed summary of works in which the measure is applied to recognition. The works which employed the examined similarity measure are collected and reported chronologically, in order to have an overview on how the research changed over the time. After this part, each similarity measure is compared to others depending on the algorithms, recognition rate, and computational cost. Contributions that contain information about performances of these measures of similarity and compare them to others are reported. Lastly, some conclusions are drawn.

ACKNOWLEDGEMENTS

Declared None.

CONFLICT OF INTEREST

The authors confirm that this book contents have no conflict of interest.

Enrico Vezzetti

&

Federica Marcolin

Department of Management and Production Engineering

Politecnico di Torino

Torino

Italy

E-mails: federica.marcolin@polito.it and enrico.vezzetti@polito.it

CHAPTER 1

Introduction

Abstract: Face recognition is a growing-up branch of pattern recognition in the context of image and vision. Conferences have arisen and brand new technologies have been coming to light providing more and more accurate recognition rates. But what is face recognition? The problem statement could be formulated this way: "Given still or video images of a scene, identify or verify one or more persons in the scene using a stored database of faces" [1]. Face recognition branch is core inasmuch the applications involving recognition algorithms for human face are aimed at different applications such as biometrics, authentication, identification of suspects. This chapter offers an overview of what are similarity and similarity measures.

Keywords: Similarity, similarity measure, metric, similarity function, face recognition.

CONCEPT OF SIMILARITY

"Despite the rapid advances in machine learning, in many recognition problems, the decision making relies on intuitive and basic concepts such as distance from or **similarity** to some reference patterns. This approach becomes significant when the training samples available to model a class of objects are not several. Examples belong to the context of content-based retrieval from image or video databases, where the query image is the only sample at our disposal to define the object model, or to biometrics, where only one or a few biometric traits can be acquired during subject enrolment to create a reference template. In biometric applications, identity verification is performed when a distance function measures the degree of similarity of an unknown pattern to the claimed identity template. If the degree is lower than a pre-specified threshold, the unknown pattern is rejected; otherwise it is accepted to be the same as the claimed identity. Similarity is quantified in terms of a similarity function. So, smaller the distance, the greater the similarity of two entities" [2]. More generally, similarity has been investigated in psychology field for decades. Recently, the topic has been largely reprised. "Similarity judgments are considered to be a valuable tool when the study of human perception and cognition are addressed and play a core role in the theories of human knowledge representation, behaviour, and problem solving" [3]. Similarity is described as "an organizing principle by which individuals classify objects, form concepts, and make generalizations" [3].

Enrico Vezzetti and Federica Marcolin

In the past two decades, typical similarity measures, such as distances and functions, were applied to perform face recognition. Algorithms are various, but the process is similar: these measures are computed between different face images or shells, in order to make a comparison. Data may be two-dimensional, such as jpeg images or video frames, or three-dimensional, namely obtained by intersecting more images of the same face or scanning the person with a 3D scanner.

A collection of similarity measures for face recognition is here presented. Firstly, Chapter 1 introduces the definition of similarity measure is given. Then, every measure is defined and described; its face recognition applications and comparison on recognition rates with other distances in previous works are shown. Minkowski distances are presented in Chapter 2, with sections on taxicab, Euclidean, Chebyshev distances, and performances. Mahalanobis, Hausdorff, and cosine-based distances are introduced in Chapters 3, 4, and 5, respectively, with their respective subsections on recognition rates. Bottleneck, Procrustes, earth mover's, and Bhattacharyya distances are reported in Chapter 6, while Chapter 7 and 8 deal with errors and similarity functions, respectively, although they are not considered as measures, but have been employed as measures of similarity. Chapter 9 is devoted to all other similarity measures, whose application in face recognition was minor.

For each measure whose performance in face recognition was tested and compared, a table is reported. It provides information on metric feature of the measures, namely says if it is a metric or not; reports the algorithms and methods which the measure was applied to; shows the data employed for the respective algorithms; contains recognition rate, accuracy, or percentage of the faces correctly recognized, or error. It also shows the respective bibliographical reference.

Lastly, a conclusion on measures performances completes the treatise.

SIMILARITY MEASURES

A **similarity measure** may be a distance function, a distance metric or a similarity function. "A *distance function* is a function defined over pairs of points. Given a pair of data-points, the function produces a real (and possibly bounded) value measuring the distance between them. Formally, a distance function $D: X \times X \rightarrow \Re$ assigns a real number for any pair of points from the input space $x_i, x_j \in X$" [4]. X has a dimension d.

Distance metrics are special forms of distance functions. A distance metric D maps point pairs x_i, x_j into the nonnegative reals $-D: X \times X \rightarrow \Re_+$ and obeys the following four **metric properties**:

1. non-negativity: $D(x_i, x_j) \geq 0$;
2. isolation (the so called "identity of indiscernibles"): $D(x_i, x_j) = 0$ iff $x_i = x_j$;
3. symmetry: $D(x_i, x_j) = D(x_j, x_i)$;
4. triangular inequality (or "subadditivity"): $D(x_i, x_j) + D(x_j, x_k) \geq D(x_i, x_k)$

Conditions 1 and 2 together produce positive definiteness [5]. A distance function do not necessarily meet all of these conditions. *E.g.*, if $D(x_i, x_j) = 0$ for $x_i \neq x_j$, we end up with a *pseudo-metric*. While a *semi-metric* do not satisfy the triangle inequality [6]. By descarding the property of symmetry, the term "distance function" is adopted.

"An *ultra-metric* is a distance metric which satisfies a strengthened version of the triangular inequality. In a Euclidean coordinate system, this is equivalent to require that the triangles of pairwise distances between every three points are isosceles with the unequal length no longer than the length of the two equal sides" [4] – *i.e.* for any three points $x_i, x_j, x_k \in X$

$$D(x_i, x_j) \leq \max\{D(x_i, x_k), D(x_j, x_k)\}. \tag{1.1}$$

A related concept is that of similarity function. "A *similarity function* is a function defined over pairs of points which measures the similarity (or resemblance) of the two points" [4]. Thus, a similarity function is inversely conceptualized compared to a distance function - if two points are very similar, the distance between them is small but the similarity function will have a high value. Thus, there are several ways to convert a similarity function into a distance function and viceversa. One adopted way is:

$$D(x_i, x_j) = e^{-S(x_i, x_j)}, \tag{1.2}$$

where, $D(x_i, x_j)$ is a distance function and $S(x_i, x_j)$ is a similarity function. Assuming that the similarity function lays in the range $[0,1]$, the transformation can be:

$$D(x_i, x_j) = 1 - S(x_i, x_j). \qquad (1.3)$$

“Generally, algorithms which learn distance functions are also adopted to learn similarity functions” [4].

Distance metrics work properly in contexts where their four properties hold. “However, in some cases, the “natural” distances between data-points do not conform to the metric properties. It was shown that distance functions which are robust to outliers are not metric, as they tend to violate the triangular inequality. Examples of these kinds of distance functions are common in machine vision. In this field, many times images are part-based compared. Also, human similarity judgments often violate both the symmetry and triangular inequality metric properties. In other contexts, it is sometimes the “identity of indiscernibles” to be violated. For example the optimal distance function for nearest-neighbour classification and the family of binary distance functions violate this property” [4].

Furthermore, in many cases it is requested that a similarity measure meet some continuity properties and the property of invariance.

“The following four properties are about robustness, a form of **continuity**; for instance, they are useful to be robust against discretization effects:

- perturbation robustness: for each $\varepsilon > 0$, there is an open set F of deformations sufficiently close to the identity, such that $d(f(A), A) < \varepsilon$ for all $f \in F$. For instance, a distance function can be requested to be robust against small affine distortion;

- crack robustness: for each each $\varepsilon > 0$, and each “crack” x in *bd(A)*, the boundary of A, an open neighbourhood U of x exists such that for all B, $A - U = B - U$ implies $d(A, B) < \varepsilon$;

- blur robustness: for each $\varepsilon > 0$, an open neighbourhood U of *bd(A)* exists, such that $d(A, B) < \varepsilon$ for all B satisfying $B - U = A - U$ and $bd(A) \subseteq bd(B)$;

- noise and occlusion robustness: for each $x \in \Re^2 - A$, and each $\varepsilon > 0$, an open neighbourhood U of x exists such that for all B, $B - U = A - U$ implies $d(A,B) < \varepsilon$;

A distance function d is **invariant** under a chosen group of transformations G if for all $g \in G$, $d\left(g(x_i), g(x_j)\right) = d\left(x_i, x_j\right)$ [7]. In the context of recognition, the similarity measure is often desired to be invariant under affine transformations.

Having decided upon a feature space to represent facial information, the next issue that needs to be addressed is what similarity measure to use within that feature space. Several candidate metrics have been studied in the face-recognition literature and in the following chapters, a summary of the main approaches is presented [8]. The presentation of these similarity measures starts with the most commonly used distance metric: the Minkowski distance.

CHAPTER 2

Minkowski Distances for Face Recognition

Abstract: Minkowski distances really deserve a whole chapter for theirselves. Depending on the value choice of parameter p, explained here below in the introduction, the concept of Minkowski distance is split up in different distance measures, which are typically known as taxicab (*p=1*), Euclidean (*p=2*), and Chebyshev distances ($p = \infty$). These measures have been widely employed in the 2D face recognition context, as the section dealing with performances outlines.

Keywords: Minkowski distance, taxicab distance, city block distance, Manhattan distance, Euclidean distance, Chebyshev distance.

PREVIOUS WORK

The **Minkowski distance** is a generalized form of other well-known distances, also known as $L_p - norm$. It is a metric but, differently from other metrics, its definition is based on a free parameter p ($p > 0$), to be set. This distance is

$$D_{Minkowski}\left(x_i, x_j\right) = \sqrt[p]{\sum_{k=1}^{d} \left|x_{ik} - x_{jk}\right|^p} . \quad (2.1)$$

When $p = 1$ it yields the so-called taxicab distance; for $p = 2$ it is the Euclidean distance; for $p = \infty$, the Chebyshev distance is obtained. Nonetheless, different values for p can be picked [4]. For all $p > 1$, the L_p distances are metrics. For $p < 1$ it is not a metric anymore, as the triangle inequality concept is not met [7].

The Minkowski distance is the most popular distance measuring, not only in face recognition field, but also generally. Huet worked on object recognition *via* hierarchical methods, in which objects are represented by line patterns from large structural libraries. Having established representation means for a rapid indexing algorithms, some measures are presented in order to indicate the similarity between line-patterns. Two Minkowski distances are considered [9].

Draper, Yambor, and Beveridge used Principal Component Analysis (PCA) aimed to face recognition for examining the role of Eigenspace distances and Eigenvectors. Among the different distance measures employed, also two Minkowski distances are used [10].

Enrico Vezzetti and Federica Marcolin

Kittler, Ghaderi, Windeatt, and Matas applied Error Correcting Output coding (ECOC) classifier on a new method for face verification. Different signals are represented by ECOC codes, which are distinguished from each other once they pass through a corruption transmission channel. Distances are then measured using Minkowski distance [11-13].

Liu and Wechsler introduced Gabor-Fisher Classifier (GFC), using two Minkowski distances as similarity measures. In order to cope face expressions and illumination changes, advisable face features relying on frequency, position, and orientation in the space domain are derived by Gabor wavelets. Fractional power polynomial models are included *via* the extension of Kernel PCA (KPCA) approach aimed to enhance the accurateness. For comparison purposes, similarity measures are introduced. Furthermore, they introduced the variant version of the Minkowski distance, namely the **weighted Minkowski distance** function, in which weights are introduced to select features importance:

$$D_{weighted\_Minkowski}\left(x_i, x_j\right) = \sqrt[p]{\sum_{k=1}^{d} w_k \left|x_{ik} - x_{jk}\right|^p}, \tag{2.2}$$

where, $w_k, k = 1,...,p$ are the weights applied to different features. Has said previously, d is the length of vectors x_i and x_j [14-16].

Perlibakas used Minkowski as a distance measure to test face recognition performance of PCA-based approach [17].

Zhao adapted machine learning techniques for keystroke authentication. Distances between patterns are extracted and the Minkowski distance is computed [18].

Park, An, Jeong, Kang, and Pankoo proposed the use of colour correlograms on multi-resolution images for image classification. The multi-resolution correlogram matching is performed by first computing distances between similarly-'resolutioned' correlograms. Then, these distances are weighted and adopted as similarity measures to recoup similar images. The distances between probe and gallery images are quantified with the Minkowski distance [19]. Liu, Zhang, Lu, and Ma provided a literature review of the recent technical achievements in semantic image retrieval. Minkowski-type metric is presented as one of the most employed similarity measure to define region distance [20].

Smith employed it to study the efficiency of various feature extraction techniques, such as Local Binary Patterns (LBP) and Linear Discriminant Analysis (LDA) [8]. Furthermore, he used it as a similarity measure to study angular LDA and Support Vector Machine (SVM) ensembles in face recognition applications [21].

Sadeghi, Samiei, and Kittler dealt with fusing PCA- and LDA-based similarity measures aimed at face verification. They investigated a variety of metrics, including two Minkowski distances [2, 22].

Omaia and Batista presented a recognition method for frontal human faces on grey-scale images. The Discrete Cosine Transform (DCT) of the query face and of the faces of the database is computed. Then, a distance obtained as the sum of the differences between the modules of DCT coefficients is evaluated. The faces with the shortest distances belong to the same person. The order-one Minkowski metric (taxicab distance) was adopted to compute distances between face coefficients, turning to be simple and efficient [23].

Cai, Wang, and Xu presented a new image distance for Kernel Fisher Discriminant Analysis (KFDA) aimed at face recognition and compared the outcomes with canonical similarity distances, such as Minkowski distances [24]. Rouabhia, K. Hamdaoui and Tebbikh inserted the Minkowski distance in a list of commonly used similarity measures for face recognition. In this case the scope was face images classification and recognition [25].

"Studies of cognitive psychology about human perception of similarity show that humans infer similarity relying on the aspects that are similar among the compared objects, rather than on the dissimilar ones. From this point of view, the similarity based on classical Minkowski distance, which incorporates all aspects of the compared objects, is questionable" [26]. Yan, Liu, Lu, and Ma proposed **Dynamic Partial Function** (DPF), a modified form of Minkowski metric, to solve the above problem. Firstly, they assumed Δd_ks to be ordered as $\Delta d_1 \le \Delta d_2 \le \ldots \le \Delta d_n$. DPF is defined as

$$D_{DPF}(u,v) = \left(\frac{1}{m} \sum_{k=1}^{m} \Delta d_k^p \right)^{1/p}, \tag{2.3}$$

where, u and v are two image feature vectors with n elements, $m \le n$ is the number of core components in the quantification of similarity. Differently from Minkowski, "DPF dynamically selects the subset of most similar features for a given pair of images, and computes the similarity based on it" [26]. Thus, it acts similarly to human visual perception. They also conducted face recognition experiments using this distance. The same measure was also employed by Liu, Zhang, Lu, and Ma [20].

Since, Minkowski distance remains undefined until the parameter p is not set, it is better to introduce the most common and famous Minkowski distances: taxicab distance, Euclidean distance, and Chebyshev distance. Their applications in face recognition fields will be also presented.

TAXICAB DISTANCE

The **Taxicab distance**, approached by Hermann Minkowski in XIX century, is given by the sum of the absolute differences of the coordinates of the two points between which the distance is computed. It is alternatively called **rectilinear distance**, $L_1 - norm$, **city block distance** or **Manhattan distance**, which is its most famous name. The names allude to the squared grid layout of Manhattan streets. As a matter of fact, the taxicab distance is the shortest path a car takes to go from one cross of the borough to another. It is shown in Fig. (**1**).

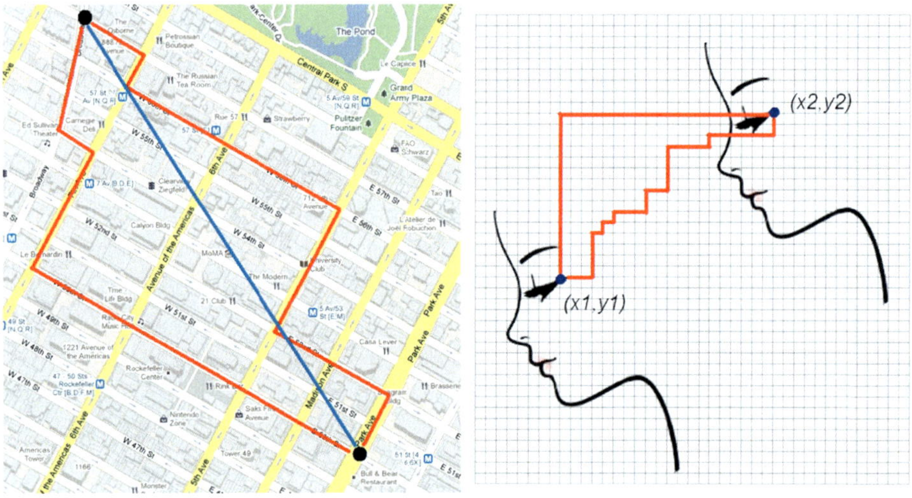

Figure 1: (Left) Taxicab geometry (red lines) *versus* Euclidean distance (blue line). In taxicab geometry the two pictured lines have the same length (12 blocks) for the same route. In Euclidean geometry, the blue line has length $6\times\sqrt{2} \approx 8.48$, and is the unique shortest path. (Although it is not true in the picture, we assume that city blocks have all equal length.) (Right) Two possible taxicab distances between corresponding points (x_1, y_1) and (x_2, y_2) on two 2D faces on a grid. Grids and face data may also be three-dimensional. The figure is reported two-dimensional for the sake of simplicity.

It is defined this way:

$$D_{Taxicab}\left(x_i, x_j\right) = \sum_{k=1}^{d} \left| x_{ik} - x_{jk} \right|. \tag{2.4}$$

"The distance measures the shortest path (in "city blocks") to be 'walked' between the two points x_i and x_j if a city is laid out in square blocks. More formally, it is the sum of the lengths of the projections of the line segments between the points onto the coordinate axes of the coordinate system" [4].

For its simplicity, it is widely used for the similarity of faces. Artiklar, Hassoun, and Watta presented a shifted input patterns algorithm to be adopted in pattern recognition systems. A pattern recognition scheme produces an ordered output list, ranked according to similarity to an input pattern. They used a simple Nearest Neighbour (NN) classification scheme and ranked outputs relying on city block distance in the case of grey-scale images [27].

Draper, Yambor, and Beveridge examined the role of Eigenspace distance measures on face recognition methods based on PCA. City block distance was inserted in a combination of four classic distances, with the hypothesis that this combination might outperform the individual distance measures [10]. O'Toole, Cheng, Phillips, Ross, and Wild looked at how humans processed individual faces to evaluate the consistency of computational algorithms. Through a comparison between the similarity measures generated by different recognition techniques and by human perception, they assessed the accord between computer and human. The algorithms were all PCA-based facial representations and only differ for the adopted similarity measures. Taxicab distance was one of the used similarity measures [28].

Beveridge, She, Draper, and Givens reviewed some major issues related to the statistical evaluation of Human Identification algorithms. Gallery images are ranked according to similarity to a specific probe image. In particular, city-block distance is given as an example of similarity measure for PCA algorithms [29]. As said previously, Kittler, Ghaderi, Windeatt, and Matas developed a method for face verification which relies on Error Correcting Output Coding (ECOC). To train a binary classifier set, the client set is over and over split up into two ECOC subsets (super-classes). The output determines ECOC feature space, in which converted patterns of bilkers are isolated from innocents' ones. First order Minkowski metric (taxicab distance) is adopted instead of Euclidean, so that outliers are more robust [11, 13]. By proposing GFC, Liu and Wechsler applied the Enhanced Fisher linear discriminant Model (EFM) to an improved Gabor feature vector gained by standard Gabor wavelet facial formalization. To evaluate the efficiency of the various representation and recognition methods, different similarity measures were adopted, including $L_1 - norm$ [14-16].

Jiao, Gao, Chen, Cui, and Shan adopted a local feature analysis approach. Local features are firstly localized *via* face structure knowledge and grey-scale distribution information. Then, face is represented by Gabor jets on these feature points and their spatial distances. In order to measure the distance in the feature space, some metrics are adopted, including city block distance [30].

Ebrahimpour presented fractal methods for recognition, including face recognition. Geometrical and luminance descriptors are selected in the probe grey-scale images *via* fractal code. Given that these codes are not univocal, it is possible to change fractal parameters set without crucial quality changes to the new image. "Fractal image set coding keeps geometrical parameters the same for all images in the database. Differences between images are captured in the non-geometrical or luminance parameters, which are the faster to be computed. For recognition purposes, the fractal code of a probe image is applied to all the images in the training set for one iteration" [31], and similarity distances are computed between the two. City block distance appears among the employed similarity measures. Later, he presented and ensemble based techniques for face recognition. He adopted *k* Nearest Neighbours (*k*NN) as main classification technique and Bagging as wrapping classification method. *k*NN is an extension of the simple NN classifier system. NN classifier works on a simple nonparametric decision. The nearest neighbour is the image in the training database with the minimum distance of its features from the features of query image. The set of measures adopted include city block distance [32]. Arodź adopted Radon transform properties – scaling, rotation-in-plane, and translation – for deriving a transformation which could be invariant to spatial image variations, and that could use direct translation, angle representation, and 1D Fourier transform, in order to ease recognition task. Manhattan distance was evaluated as similarity measure [33].

Yang, Gao, Zhang, and Yang formulated a two-phase kernel Independent Component Analysis (ICA) algorithm in the "kernel-inducing feature space", *i.e.* whitened KPCA plus ICA. "Kernel PCA spheres data and makes the data structure become as linearly separable as possible through an implicit nonlinear mapping determined by kernel". For each method, one-hundred characteristics are extracted to feature all facial images. A NN classifier with various similarity measures is adopted for image retrieval. City block is used both in PCA and KPCA methods [34]. Zhao adapted machine learning techniques for keystroke authentication, *i.e.* an access control system to identify legitimate users through their typing behaviour. Manhattan distance was computed between different patterns for the whole elapsed pattern duration and used as similarity measure [18]. Delac, Grgic, and their co-authors provided an overview of the most significant statistical subspace methods for face recognition, in which the city block distance was cited as a similarity distance [1]. Later, they investigated the potential of undertaking verification within the JPEG and JPEG2000 compressed domain. Through a new comparison methodology they showed that facial verification could be successfully computationally fulfilled directly into these compressed domains. The $L_1 - norm$ for PCA was adopted as a distance metric in the calculated subspaces [35].

Matta and Dugelay described an identity recognition approach in video sequences by exploiting "behavioural information of head dynamics and displacement signals of head features". Taxicab metric is computed for each colour component. Thus, the obtained measures are added *via* equal component weighting [36]. Shi, Samal and Marx evaluated how biologically-significant facial landmarks and their geometry could be processed for facial verification *via* PCA. The performances of three distance metrics were investigated, including the $L_1 - norm$ [37]. Yampolskiy and Govindaraju proposed a suitable similarity function for behavioural biometric systems and compared its performance on a newly-developed matching algorithm to that of other metrics, including the Manhattan distance [38]. Then, they proposed a literature review in behavioural biometrics related to "skills, style, preference, knowledge, motor-skills, and approaches of people while accomplishing different everyday tasks such as driving car, talking on the phone, or using laptop". In this work, Manhattan distance is considered among the most significant similarity measures [39].

Graves and Nagarajah worked on multi-class classification by introducing a modified monotonic function framework to quantify the uncertainty of new observations. This approach, which works on the conversion of the input pattern vector associated to each classification set, seems to be effective in biometrics applications. "The similarity between each input pattern vector and each class is established *via* separate, monotonic, single-output neural networks". The proposed algorithm was tested with publicly available facial databases. Every input pattern vector was transformed into a new data space according to a mapping function with respect to each class. The adopted similarity functions were linearly proportional to Manhattan distances and other similarity distances [40].

Chen applied "decision level fusion of local features" to a new feature extraction method. The query face is firstly split up into reduced regions from which LBP information are extrapolated. The experiments were conducted by identifying block size, weights, and distance classifiers on different facial databases, so that specific suitable LBPs are selected for classification purpose. Then, this LBP is investigated "from perspective of information fusion scheme". The LBP-based feature set is fed to Histogram Intersection (HI) classifier. Another set is formed by extrapolating statistical features from local regions after the splitting up process and then forwarded to Manhattan distance classifier [41]. Sadeghi, Samiei, and Kittler addressed the issue of selecting and fusing eight similarity measures-based classifiers for face recognition in a LDA feature space. The taxicab distance is included [2, 22].

Dawwd and Mahmood introduced a "dynamically reconfigurable hardware model for Convolutional Neural Network (CNN)". The "modular prototyping system" relies on XILINX FPGAs and emulates CNN hardware implementation for face recognition. The similarity distance choice is a key point influencing hardware implementation of convolutional node. Taxicab distance is adopted to measure the similarity between the features extracted. In particular, taxicab distance is used to avoid multiplications involved in the computation of the L_2 norm, which is said to be the most critical operation in hardware. The implementation of this distance requires "absoluter, subtractor, and accumulator". Dot product is avoided and multiplier is not required [42]. Orozco-Alzate and Castellanos-Domínguez proposed a survey of prototype-based classification. "It ranges from the classical NN classifier to the nearest feature space classifier, including also modifications of the distance measure and several editing and condensing methods". A framework of dissimilarity representations and classifications is detailed, as for the NN identification a distance measure is to be defined. Manhattan distance is adopted both for interpretability and computational convenience [43]. Izmailov and Krzyżak improved eigenface-based systems, in terms of robustness, taking also into consideration illumination/pose/background changes. They proposed a "face cropping and alignment" method, which was integrated into the Eigenface algorithm. They also investigated how several metrics – including Manhattan distance – could affect overall system performance [44].

EUCLIDEAN DISTANCE

The most intuitive, significant, and widely adopted distance metric is the **Euclidean distance**, defined by:

$$D_{Euclidean}\left(x_i, x_j\right) = \sqrt[2]{\sum_{k=1}^{d} \left|x_{ik} - x_{jk}\right|^2} \ . \qquad (2.5)$$

It is also known as the L_2 distance or the squared $L_2 - norm$ [4]. It is commonly intended as the distance "as the crow flies". It is shown in Fig. (**2**).

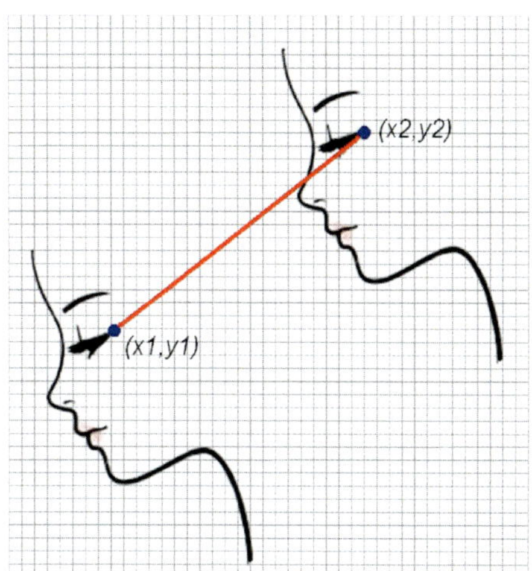

Figure 2: Euclidean distance between points (x_1, y_1) and (x_2, y_2) of two faces on grid. Similarly, it can be done in 3D.

Because of its immediacy, it is the most used ever for all application genres. Consequently, this distance is also very employed as a similarity measure for face recognition purposes. Turk and Pentland presented a face detection and identification method. Then, a "near-real-time" face verification method was introduced which tracks human head and identifies the query person *via* comparison with facial features of those individuals belonging to the gallery set. Eigenfaces, namely eigenvectors of facial set, define facial space. To state which facial class offers the most accurate representation for a probe face, the face class is identified that minimizes the Euclidean distance between face classes [45].

Gordon explored face recognition from a feature-based representation extracted from range images. A vector of feature descriptors represents faces; the comparison between two of them is performed *via* their relationship in the feature space. The vector formed by the set of descriptor values for a probe face places it in the space of all possible faces. To adopt this representation for recognition it is required that the all the points in feature space corresponding to the same person will cluster with regard to some similarity measure. The Euclidean distance is adopted. Once the feature vectors are calculated, for any query face the distance between the target point in feature space and the other points in the database is computed. Each face was used as target, thus calculating all distances between every two vectors in the feature space, stored in a symmetric matrix. The best match for a target is found by sorting the entries, in increasing order, in the row of the matrix corresponding to the target; it is given by the column with the smallest distance [46].

Lipoščak and Loncaric adopted scale-space filtering for profile images. A grey-scale profile image is thresholded to gain a binary b/w image. A pre-processing phase outlines the front curve of the silhouette that bounds the facial image, from which 12 key points are automatically detected using scale-space filtering by varying the scale parameter and a set of twenty-one features is derived from these points. After feature normalization, the Euclidean distance is adopted to quantify the similarity of the feature vectors derived from the outline profiles [47].

Draper, Yambor, and Beveridge compared different similarity measures over the Moon and Phillips's FERET database and investigated alternative approaches for selecting sub-sets of Eigenvectors in face recognition systems based on PCA. They tested a summation of distance measures, including squared Euclidean distance [10]. O'Toole, Cheng, Phillips, Ross, and Wild used Euclidean distance to evaluate the reliability of face processing computational methods by analysing the way both algorithms and humans processed human faces [28].

Liu and Wechsler described a Gabor Feature Classifier to be applied to face recognition, where the Euclidean distance is used as similarity measure [14-16].

Jiao, Gao, Chen, Cui, and Shan used Euclidean distance as a similarity measure for a face recognition approach relying on local feature analysis [30].

Moreno, Sánchez, Vélez, and Díaz analyzed the discriminating power of 3D descriptors extracted from three-dimensional human facial surfaces. They performed a *HK* segmentation to isolate areas characterized by prominent curvature, relying on the signs of mean and Gaussian curvatures *H* and *K*. The matching procedure was based on the minimum Euclidean distance classifier [48].

Xu, Wang, Tan, and Quan represented scattered 3D facial point clouds with a regular mesh adopting hierarchical mesh fitting. Then, local shape variation information and global geometric features are extracted to mark out the person. The matching process is not time consuming, as it only involves the computation of Euclidean distance between pairs of points in a low dimensional space [49]. Ebrahimpour and Kouzani presented an ensemble-based classifier approach for face recognition. The similarity is measured with some distances including Euclidean one [32]. Ebrahimpour also used it for fractal methods for human face recognition [31]. Arodź evaluated the Euclidean distance as a similarity measure for a face recognition procedure based on Radon transform [33].

Arandjelović and Cipolla were interested in face recognition using video sequences. The recognition framework is realistic and unconstrained; lighting, pose, and user motion pattern have a wide variability and facial images are of low resolution. They proposed to use the Euclidean distance as a dissimilarity measure between normalized cluster centres [50, 51].

Lee, Song, Yang, Shin, and Sohn proposed facial feature extraction-based procedure for three-dimensional face recognition using geometrical features. They extracted three curvatures and eight invariant facial feature points. The features are directly applied to depth-based Dynamic Programming (DP) and a feature-based SVM. In order to extrapolate feature values of library and query data, Euclidean distance is adopted as similarity measure to identify similar face candidates [52]. Hüsken, Brauckmann, Gehlen, and Von der Malsburg discussed different approaches and their expected advantages for fusing bi-dimensional and three-dimensional face verification. In particular, Hierarchical Graph Matching (HGM), a known method for bi- and three-dimensional facial identification, was evaluated. Euclidean distances between feature vectors are adopted to evaluate the similarity between faces [53]. Wang, Zhang, and Feng introduced a modified Euclidean distance for images, the Image Euclidean Distance (IMED). "Unlike the standard Euclidean distance, IMED takes into account the spatial relationships of pixels. Thus, it is robust to small perturbation". Then, IMED is applied to face verification. Its main strength seems to be its applicability to SVM, LDA, PCA, and other image classification techniques. [54]. Delac, Grgic, and Liatsis described three appearance-based statistical approaches, PCA, ICA, and LDA. Euclidean distance is used to select which facial class offers the best representation of the probe facial image [1]. Yang, Gao, Zhang, and Yang formulated developed a "two-phase kernel ICA algorithm", *i.e.* KPCA plus ICA. Euclidean distance metric is adopted both in PCA and KPCA methods [34]. Zhao explored keystroke authentication and adopted Euclidean distance as similarity measure together with the Manhattan distance [18].

Bronstein, Bronstein, and Kimmel successfully "proposed to model facial expressions as isometries of the facial surface". The newly developed 3DFACE face recognition method successfully extracts expression-invariant signatures relying on isometry-invariant face representation. A crucial step of the process is the embedding of the facial geometrical structure into a Euclidean flat space. They replaced the flat embedding by a spherical one in order to build 'spherical canonical images', *i.e.* new isometric invariant face representations. They introduced a dissimilarity measure "to compute the invariants between the spherical canonical images" based on the weighted Euclidean norm [55]. Later, they computed the similarity function between two surfaces in the canonical forms (CF) algorithm with the canonical Euclidean distance [56].

Senaratne and Halgamuge were inspired by Elastic Bunch Graph Matching and Active Shape Model when adopted "landmark model matching" for developing a new automatic face recognition method. "Landmark model matching consists of four phases: creation of the landmark distribution model, face finding, landmark finding, recognition". Previously, in the verification step, the weights assigned to each landmark or to other key points were set through experimentation. These weights have been optimized. Euclidean distance was suggested to evaluate the reliability of the "face finding" step [57]. Shi, Samal and Marx adopted "landmarks and their geometry to reduce the search space for the face verification process". Euclidean distance was used as a similarity measure [37]. Niennattrakul and Ratanamahatana demonstrated how multimedia data, such as video, images and audio, could be reduced to time series representations, namely a more compact form, without losing significant features. This method is applicable to object tracking in videos, voice/face/profile recognition and classification, and fingerprinting. Similarly to standard clustering algorithms, time series clustering assembles similar objects into groups. Thus, its efficiency fully depends on clustering algorithm itself and on the chosen similarity distance. They focused on Euclidean distance [58]. Matta and Dugelay proposed a recognition method "based on displacement signals of head features" extrapolated from a video frame. The head movement is took into exam by retrieving eyes, nose, and mouth displacements in every video sequence. The similarity measure is built by adding the L_2 norms calculated for each colour component [36].

Yampolskiy and Govindaraju introduced a new similarity measure for behavioural biometric systems. In order to show "its superiority with respect to the chosen domain, [they] compared the performance of a newly introduced matching algorithm to that of other well-known similarity distances with respect to strategy-based behavioural biometrics". They outlined a collection of the most significant similarity measures adopted within the context of biometric applications. Then, they introduced their new similarity measures; the Euclidean distance was adopted in the performance comparison [38]. They also inserted it in a survey of behavioural biometrics [39].

Gupta, Aggarwal, Markey, and Bovik introduced a systematic procedure for selecting key points associated with diverse facial structural features. They calculated the final distance between faces in LDA space using the Euclidean metric [59]. Park, An, Jeong, Kang, and Pankoo proposed the use of colour correlograms on multi-resolution images. They used Euclidean distance between query and gallery image [19]. Graves and Nagarajah employed mapping functions of the degree-of-similarity, linearly proportional to the Euclidean metric, for face recognition [40].

Gizatdinova and Surakka developed an expression-invariant feature-based landmarking method from static face images. The performance of different facial feature detectors was expressed "in terms of either visual inspection of the detection result or error measure computed as a distance between manually annotated and automatically detected landmark locations". The error measure is obtained as the Euclidean pixel distance. So, "the fewer pixels there are, the better the accuracy of the feature detector". "This point measure is sufficient for all applications which can make use of a single pixel point result as an output of the feature detector" [60]. Tunçer introduced a 3D face representation and recognition method relying on spherical harmonics expansion. The input data is the range image of the face and is called 2.5 dimensional. The human face is modelled as two concentric half ellipses for the selection of region of interest. Marker points are used in 3D to register the faces so that the nose point tip is at the origin and the line across the two eyes lies parallel to the horizontal plane. A PCA-based component analysis is done to further align the faces vertically. The aligned face is stitched and mapped to an ellipsoid and transformed using real spherical harmonics expansion. Euclidean distance is adopted as a measure of similarity between reduced feature vectors [61]. Chen outlined a detailed analysis of optimal parameter selection in LBP algorithm. Then, a decision level fusion scheme is introduced to improve the performance by merging information extracted from both local texture patterns and LBP labels. Euclidean distance is adopted as a similarity metric [41].

Sadeghi, Samiei, and Kittler dealt with fusing eight similarity measures for face verification purposes, including the Euclidean distance [2, 22].

Orozco-Alzate and Castellanos-Domínguez investigated various measures with the Eigenface method, including squared L_2 norm, in the forms of Sum Square Error, weighted Sum Squared Error, and Mean Square Error [43].

Klare, Mallapragada, Jain, and Davis proposed an image clustering ad visualization framework for face carvings at archaeological sites. The similarity between couples of faces are evaluated *via* Procrustes analysis on local facial zones such as eyes, nose, and mouth calculating the weighted Euclidean distance. Different weights were assigned to the facial components [62]. Ober, Neugebauer, and Sallee investigated the utility of one-dimensional anthropometric measurements as a biometric for face recognition when the subject pose differs in query and gallery data. They used a large three-dimensional full-body dataset with multiple poses per subject. They also used Euclidean distance and normalized Euclidean distance for the similarity score [63]. Cai, Wang, and Xu listed some similarity measures for face recognition, including Euclidean distance and IMED [24].

More recently, Euclidean distance was employed as deviation, *i.e.* error, between test and training sample for developing two new classification/recognition algorithms applied to face recognition. Xu, Zhu, Chen, and Pan proposed an improved version of the NN classifier method [64], while Yang, Liu, Wu, Li, and Wang introduced another version of the Collaboration Representation-based Classification (CNC), the CNC with reduced residual [65].

CHEBYSHEV DISTANCE

The **Chebyshev distance** (or **Tchebychev distance**) between two points is "the maximum distance between the points in any single dimension" [4]:

$$D_{Chebyshev}\left(x_i, x_j\right) = \max_k \left|x_{ik} - x_{jk}\right|. \tag{2.6}$$

This distance is a particular case of the L_∞ norm [4] and is also known as **chessboard distance**, as "in the game of chess the minimum number of moves needed by a king to go from one square to another equals the Chebyshev distance between the square centres. It holds if the squares have side length one, as represented in bi-dimensional spatial coordinates with axes aligned to the chessboard edges” [66]. For instance, in Fig. (**3**), the Chebyshev distance between F6 and E2 equals 4.

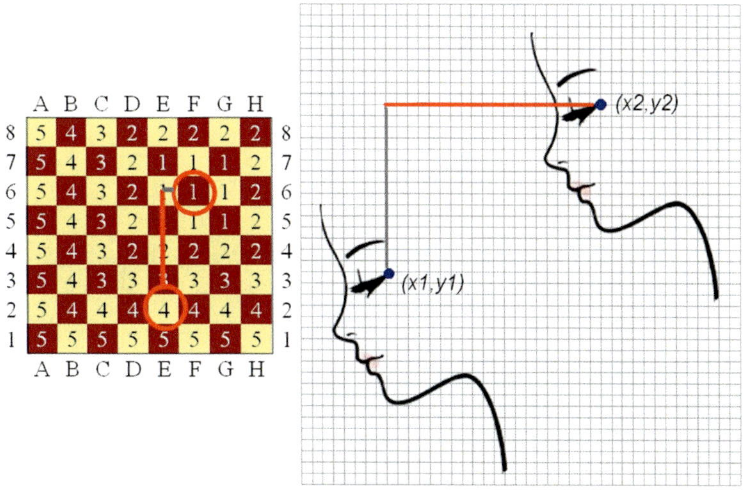

Figure 3: (Left) A chessboard. The Chebyshev distance (red-coloured) between two spaces “gives the minimum number of moves a king is to move between them. This is because a king can move diagonally, so that the jumps to cover the smaller distance parallel to a rank or column is absorbed into the jumps covering the larger” [66]. (Right) Chebyshev distance (red-coloured) between corresponding point of two faces on grid. Grey segment was not chosen as Chebyshev distance because is shorter than the red one. Similarly, 3D data may be used.

Although it is not very common, some researchers employed it for face recognition. Ebrahimpour employed Chebyshev distance for fractal methods for human face recognition [31].

Trias evaluated well-known face verification approaches, such as PCA, ICA and LDA, on classical databases. The Chebyshev distance, together with other distances, is used as a measure of similarity and dissimilarity [67].

Cohen-Steiner, Edelsbrunner, and Harer dealt with comparing and classifying geometric shapes. The approach consists in associating each shape with a basic signature, so that two congruent shapes have the same signature. The $L_\infty - norm$ is used to measure the distances between signatures [68].

Graves and Nagarajah proposed a modified “monotonic function model to estimate the uncertainty associated with a new observation” in the context of multi-class classification for biometric recognition. Chebyshev metric was chosen in order to reduce computational complexity [40].

Sadeghi, Samiei, and Kittler fused eight similarity measures for face verification purposes, including the Chebyshev distance [2, 22].

Orozco-Alzate and Castellanos-Domínguez said Chebyshev distance is convenient as a similarity measure for face recognition, not just for both interpretability and computational convenience [43].

OTHER MINKOWSKI DISTANCES

Although the Minkowski distance is no longer a metric with $p < 1$, this treatment would be incomplete if this particular and rare Minkowski distance is not taken into consideration. It is not very common in face recognition literature. Sim, Sukthankar, Mullin, and Baluja showed that a simple memory- and appearance-based face recognition method for visitor identification could outperform more sophisticated approaches adopting PCA and neural networks. Their experiments indicated that the best performance was achieved with the Minkowski similarity distance for $p \leq 1$. The $L_0 - norm$ similarity distance is even considered one of the best choices [69]:

$$D_{L_0}(x_i, x_j) = \lim_{p \to 0^+} D_{L_p}(x_i, x_j) \tag{2.7}$$

Later, Yilmaz and Artiklar compared $L_{0.5}$, L_1, and L_2 norms in the face recognition context for 2D grey-scale face images [70].

PERFORMANCES

Minkowski distances are surely the most applied similarity measures, not only in face recognition, but generally in several recognition fields, such as objects' and images'. It was proved that the taxicab distance is less sensitive to noise than other measures, while the Euclidean distance is sensitive to deformations and translations [54]. The Euclidean distance also has a high computational cost, equal to $L_{0.5}$ distance's, while taxicab takes half time than Euclidean [70]. The Chebyshev distance is particularly known for its low computational cost [40, 43].

Liu and Wechsler evaluated the efficiency of different recognition and representation methods using **Euclidean**, **taxicab distance**, and **cosine similarity measure**. Both EFM and Fisher methods adopted the L_2 distance measure. The experiments exploit Gabor wavelet representation, using the L_1, L_2, and cosine similarity measures. The L_1, L_2, and cosine metrics are compared at different down-sampling rates. Results showed that 1) with the cosine similarity measures, "the Gabor features carry more discriminating information than how PCA features do", 2) "the performance with the three similarity measures varies less drastically". Generally, their results show that (i) the recognition rate is largely enhanced, and (ii) Mahalanobis and L_1 distances perform better than the other two. When PCA is tested, Mahalanobis distance was compared to these measures. It achieved the best percentage [14-16].

Arodź used the Radon transform properties to help face recognition with the NN decision rule. **Euclidean** and **Manhattan** metrics, and the **Tanimoto** dissimilarity measure are evaluated. Given that "the Radon transform computation of 256×256 image is time consuming, the method has been applied to images downsized to 64×64 and 32×32". Tanimoto and Euclidean distances allowed for higher recognition rate than taxicab one [33].

Yilmaz and Artiklar compared $L_{0.5}$, L_1, and L_2 **metrics** for face recognition in two-dimensional grey-scale face images. They showed that taxicab performs similarly to the other two distances "but takes almost half time to process images". They partitioned the database into sub-sets of 200, 400, and 600 people and used NN algorithm in classification tests. With 200 subjects, $L_{0.5}$ performs 92.4%, which is better than the other two with around 1% margin. With 400, all the three metrics reaches good performances and, with 600, Manhattan distance slightly outperforms the other two with 88.5%. "In terms of recognition performance, none of the 3 metrics clearly outperformed the other two in all cases". By looking at computational time, taxicab metric seems faster, as it "requires a less time to process a test image". Nonetheless, "Euclidean distance has analytical properties that make it suitable for the cases where algorithm developments require extensive math", which explains why this distance is quite popularly used. They showed through extensive simulations that, for face verification problems, L_2 and $L_{0.5}$ norms "take almost the same times to process an input image" and their effects on classification performance are also very similar, while taxicab requires almost half time compared to the other two. The effect of Manhattan metric on the global performance is a little worse than the other two in most cases but the difference is tiny. This aspect of the taxicab distance "would make it very appropriate for real-time applications" [70].

Wang, Zhang, and Feng presented a new Euclidean distance for images, the **IMED**. Two sets of experiments were conducted. The aim of the first was to compute this distance "with several other image metrics in terms of recognition rate using a NN classifier". The second block of experimentations was "to test whether embedding IMED in an image recognition technique could improve the accuracy". The compared measures are **tangent distance**, **Hausdorff distance**, and **fuzzy image metric** (FIM). The recognition results showed that IMED outperformed all the other distances except for the tangent distance, that is robust to variations. When they particularly dealt with face recognition, they tested the recognition accuracy of the new distance embedding it in PCA method and Bayesian similarity method. These approaches embedded with IMED outperformed the standard ones, respectively. Although there are several other L_2 -based measures for images ("for every symmetric and positive definite matrix", a Euclidean distance could be defined), they "often provide counter intuitive results". For instance, the standard Euclidean distance is sensitive to deformation and translation "due to the lack of consideration of pixel spatial relationship". IMED overcomes this defect [54].

Niennattrakul and Ratanamahatana evaluated the accuracy of **Euclidean distance**, **DTW**, and **histogram intersection distance** in a cluster algorithm for face image recognition. DTW outperforms Euclidean metric in all domains. Both these measures gave higher accuracy than histogram intersection distance [58].

Yampolskiy and Govindaraju compared three similarity measures (**Euclidean**, **Manhattan**, **Mahalanobis**) with the **weighted Euclidean distance**. The three distances showed very similar performances, "with Mahalanobis distance being slightly inferior to Euclidean and Manhattan distances, which showed identical performance of 12% Equal Error Rate (EER)". Weighted Euclidean distance with showed the best performance obtaining 10% EER. "A great improvement in performance of the strategy-based behavioural biometric system was observed with the inclusion of spatial information into the profiles". Once again, the weighted Euclidian distance outperformed the others, with 7% EER, while the other three similarity measures performed in the range of 9-10% EER. With the inclusion of the contextual information, the influence of the "curse of dimensionality" became evident. All performances significantly decreased. Euclidean, Mahalanobis, and Manhattan "showed an acceptable profile verification performance" with L_2 and taxicab distances being identical in terms of accuracy. Mahalanobis performed slightly worse. It could possibly be "a result of the normalization procedure which took into account variance of the data in each profile". While all similarity distances showed a high accuracy during recognition, weighted Euclidean distance slightly outperformed general methods [38].

Graves and Nagarajah tested five similarity measures for a face recognition algorithm, whose approach was given by a fusion between PCA and Fisher's LDA: **Euclidean**, **Manhattan**, **Chebyshev**, **cosine distance metric**, and **Pearson correlation coefficient**. Euclidean distance gave the best accuracy, while the Chebyshev distance metric gained a significantly lower classification performance. Thus, the choice of this metric for reducing computational complexity seems unjustified for this application [40].

Izmailov and Krzyżak investigated three similarity measures with Eigenface approach: **Euclidean**, **Manhattan**, and **Mahalanobis** distance. They showed satisfying performances in different cases, although Manhattan distance appeared to be slightly superior [44].

Cai, Wang, and Xu compared their new **IMage Matching Distance** (IMMD) with the traditional **Euclidean** and the **IMED** embedding them in a KFDA algorithm. Their method is superior than other equal methods based on Euclidean distances [24].

Low recognition rates of Minkowski distances for PCA were obtained by Liu and Wechsler [14-16]. Draper, Yambor, and Beveridge [10], Chang, Bowyer, and Flynn [71], Shi, Samal and Marx [37], who obtained better results when using Mahalanobis than Minkowski. Poor results were also obtained by Huet [9] and Yao, Wang, Lin, and Chai [72], who showed that Bhattacharyya and incremental Bhattacharyya distance, respectively, were able to perform noticeably better than the standard L_1 and L_2. Chen proved that weighted histogram intersection outperformed taxicab and Euclidean distances in LBP-based algorithm [41]. Furthermore, Sadeghi, Samiei, and Kittler obtained that Gradient Direction (GD) reached higher recognition performances than Euclidean, city block, Chebyshev distances for LDA [2, 22].

Table **1** summarizes the algorithms which Minkowski distances are employed in, recognition rates obtained in the cited articles, data type, sensitivity to noise, and computational cost.

Table 1: Features of Minkowski measures. The second column says if the measure is a metric or not; the third columns reports the algorithms and methods which the measure was applied to; the fourth column shows the type of data employed for the respective algorithms; the fifth column contains the recognition rate, or accuracy, or percentage of the faces correctly recognized, or error. The respective references are reported in the sixth column. (It is important to note that a "low" sensitivity to noise and a "low" computational cost are two good features for the measure. A quick look at the table may bring to wrong opinions).

Similarity Measure	Metric	Algorithms	Face Data Type	Dimension	Reliability (Recognition Rate)	Sensitivity to Noise	Computational Cost	References
Taxicab distance	yes	Principal Component Analysis (PCA or Eigenfaces Method)		2D	70%	Low	Medium	Liu and Wechsler [14-16]
					35% (Percent of Images Correctly Recognized)			Draper, Yambor and Beveridge in 2002 [10]
		PCA + NN		2D	65.5%			Yang, Gao, Zhang, and Yang in 2005 [34]
		Kernel PCA (KPCA) + NN		2D	64.5%			
		Improved PCA		2D	87.39%			Izmailov and Krzyżak in 2009 [44]
		PCA		2D	0.73 (Cumulative Match Score)			Shi, Samal and Marx in 2006 [37]
		PCA + Linear Discriminant Analysis (LDA)		2D	93.5%			Graves and Nagarajah in 2007 [40]
		LDA		2D	Total Error Rate in Evaluation (TEE) = 43.49; Total Error Rate Test (TET) = 50.42			Sadeghi, Samiei, and Kittler [2, 22]
		Gabor wavelets		2D	76%			Liu and Wechsler [14-16]
		Pairwise Histogram Comparison	Histograms	2D	60%			Huet in 1999 [9]
		Local binary Pattern (LBP) Method	LBP Histogram Sequences	2D	92%			Chen in 2008 [41]
		Radon Transform Properties-Based Method + NN	Images	2D	85%			Arodź in 2004 [33]
		Nearest Neighbour (NN)	Images	2D	89%		0.40 seconds (half time than Euclidean)	Yilmaz and Artiklar in 2005 [70]

Table 1: contd...

Similarity Measure	Metric	Algorithms	Face Data Type	Dimension	Reliability (Recognition Rate)	Sensitivity to Noise	Computational Cost	References
Euclidean distance	Yes	PCA		2D	43%	Medium (sensitive to deformations and translations)	High	Liu and Wechsler [14-16]
		PCA		2D	33% (Percent of Images Correctly Recognized)			Draper, Yambor and Beveridge in 2002 [10]
		PCA + NN		2D	59%			Yang, Gao, Zhang, and Yang in 2005 [34]
		KPCA + NN		2D	64.5%			Yang, Gao, Zhang, and Yang in 2005 [34]
		Improved PCA		2D	86.1%			Izmailov and Krzyżak in 2009 [44]
		PCA		2D	0.65 (Cumulative Match Score)			Shi, Samal and Marx in 2006 [37]
		PCA + LDA		2D	96.9%			Graves and Nagarajah in 2007 [40]
		LDA		2D	TEE = 36.44; TET = 44.42			Sadeghi, Samiei, and Kittler [2, 22]
		Gabor Wavelets		2D	73.5%			Liu and Wechsler [14-16]
		Clustering	Time Series Representation	2D	63.39%			Niennattrakul and Ratanamahatana in 2006 [58]
		Matching	Image Metrics	2D	83%			Cai, Wang, and Xu in 2010 [24]
		KFDA	Image Metrics	2D	88%			Cai, Wang, and Xu in 2010 [24]
		Pairwise Histogram Comparison	Histograms	2D	40%			Huet in 1999 [9]
		Local binary Pattern (LBP) Method	LBP Histogram Sequences	2D	88%			Chen in 2008 [41]
		Radon Transform Properties-Based Method + NN	Images	2D	85%			Arodź in 2004 [33]
		NN	Images	2D	89%		0.69 seconds	Yilmaz and Artiklar in 2005 [70]

Table 1: contd...

Similarity Measure	Metric	Algorithms	Face Data Type	Dimension	Reliability (Recognition Rate)	Sensitivity to Noise	Computational Cost	References
L0.5	yes	NN	Images	2D	90%	Medium	High (0.69 Seconds)	Yilmaz and Artiklar in 2005 [70]
Chebyshev Distance	yes	PCA + LDA		2D	82.3%	Medium	Low	Graves and Nagarajah in 2007 [40]
		LDA		2D	TEE = 34.27; TET = 45.17			Sadeghi, Samiei, and Kittler [2, 22]
Image Euclidean Distance (IMED)	yes	PCA		2D	73.75%	Medium	Medium	Wang, Zhang, and Feng in 2005 [54]
		Bayesian Similarity			87%			
		Matching	Image Metrics		82%			Cai, Wang, and Xu in 2010 [24]
		KFDA	Image Metrics		90%			
Image Matching Distance (IMMD)	yes	Matching	Image Metrics		93%			
		KFDA	Image Metrics		91%			

CHAPTER 3

Mahalanobis Distance for Face Recognition

Abstract: If two vectors originate from the same underlying distribution, the distance between them could be computed with the Mahalanobis distance, a generalization of the Euclidean one. Also, it can be defined as the Euclidean distance computed in the Mahalanobis space. Moreover, there exist also the city block-based Mahalanobis distance and other versions including the angle- and cosine-based ones. Largely employed for face recognition with bi-dimensional facial data, Mahalanobis gains very good performances with PCA algorithms.

Keywords: Mahalanobis distance, Mahalanobis angle, Mahalanobis cosine measure.

PREVIOUS WORK

This distance, originally proposed by Prasanta Chandra Mahalanobis in 1936 for the statistics community, relies on correlations between different features within a feature vector. The **Mahalanobis distance** is a generalized version of the Euclidean distance, which is invariant to scale and takes into account the correlations of the dataset. It is also called Mahalanobis L_2. If two vectors originate from the same underlying distribution, Mahalanobis measures the distance between them. Given a distribution p which has a covariance matrix Σ (or total scatter matrix) the Mahalanobis distance between two vectors x_i, x_j is given by:

$$D_{Mahalanobis}\left(x_i, x_j\right) = \sqrt{\left(x_i - x_j\right)^T \Sigma^{-1} \left(x_i - x_j\right)} = \sqrt{\sum_{k=1}^{d} \sum_{l=1}^{d} x_{ik} \Sigma_{lk}^{-1} x_{jl}} \,. \tag{3.1}$$

"If the covariance matrix Σ is the identity matrix, then the Mahalanobis distance becomes the Euclidean distance. If the covariance matrix is diagonal, the distance becomes normalized Euclidean" [4]. Although in its original form the Mahalanobis distance assumes that the data-points originate from a probability distribution with a covariance matrix Σ, it can be shown that the distance is well defined for any positive semi-definite (PSD) matrix A. Therefore, a general Mahalanobis matrix is often denoted by the symbol A [4]. Fig. (**4**) shows that points A and B are equally distant from the centre O of the distribution.

Enrico Vezzetti and Federica Marcolin

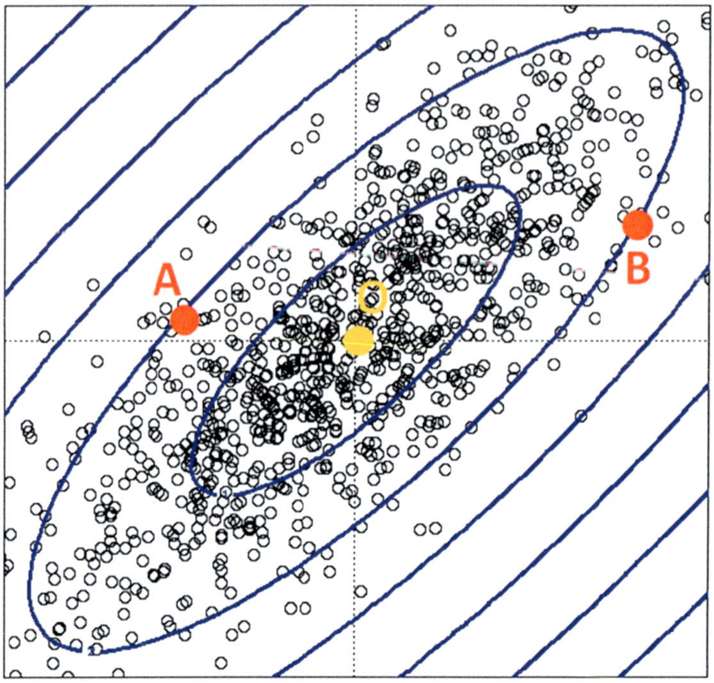

Figure 4: Contour plot of the Mahalanobis distance to the origin. *A* and *B* are at the same Euclidean distance from centre [73].

Alternatively, the Mahalanobis distance is defined as the Euclidean distance but computed in Mahalanobis space. So, for images *u* and *v* with corresponding projections *m* and *n* in Mahalanobis space, Mahalanobis L_2 is:

$$D_{Mahalanobis\_L_2}(u,v)=\sqrt{\sum_k (m_k-n_k)^2}. \quad (3.2)$$

A less famous Mahalanobis distance is the one obtained from the city block distance. It is the taxicab distance scaled to Mahalanobis space. It is called Mahalanobis L_1. So, for images *u* and *v* with corresponding projections *m* and *n* in Mahalanobis space, Mahalanobis L_1 is [74]:

$$D_{Mahalanobis\_L_1}(u,v)=\sum_k (m_k-n_k). \quad (3.3)$$

There is wide previous work on the application of this distance to face recognition. O'Toole, Cheng, Phillips, Ross, and Wild developed an approach for comparing human and computer performance for individual faces. A multidimensional representation combines the human- and model-generated similarity measures between face pairs. A Mahalanobis distance-based algorithm was included [28]. Draper, Yambor, and Beveridge worked with PCA-based face recognition systems to examine "the role of Eigenvector selection and Eigenspace distance measures" in this context. They adopted a combination of standard similarity distances, including Mahalanobis distance [10].

Liu and Wechsler introduced a Gabor-Fisher Classifier for face verification, using the Mahalanobis distance as a similarity measure [14-16].

Trias evaluated well-known face verification approaches, such as PCA, ICA and LDA, on classical databases. The Mahalanobis distance, together with other distances, is used as a measure of similarity and dissimilarity [67]. Delac, Grgic, and Liatsis gave an overview of most popular statistical subspace methods for face recognition task. Mahalanobis distance is used as a similarity measure [1].

Shi, Samal and Marx investigated how strategic landmarks extrapolated from facial images could be exploited for face verification using 2D regression. "Motivated by the Mahalanobis distance", they also introduced a method called eigenvalue weighted bi-dimensional regression, by incorporating the correlation statistics of landmarks [37, 75].

Yampolskiy and Govindaraju compared the performance of a new similarity measure with the Mahalanobis distance [38]. Then, examined current research in the field of behavioural biometrics and analysed the types of features used to describe different types of behaviours. Mahalanobis distance was employed as a similarity measure [39].

Tunçer proposed a 3D face representation and recognition method based on spherical harmonics expansion. The Mahalanobis distance is used as a similarity measure between reduced feature vectors [61].

Izmailov and Krzyżak proposed a method for detecting faces, cropping them, and performing recognition in real-time, by integrating Eigenface recognition. They also investigated the effect of various distance metrics – including Mahalanobis distance – on the overall system performance [44].

Seshandri and Savvides particularly dealt with Mahalanobis distance measure for face recognition purposes. They presented a landmarking approach in frontal face images adopting a modified Active Shape Model. Their main contributions include the study of the optimal number of facial landmarks, profiling techniques during fitting, and the conceptualization of a tailored optimization metric to determine the most accurate landmark location compared to the trivial criteria of minimization of Mahalanobis measure currently adopted. Precise landmark localization is determined by constructing profiles of neighbouring patches around candidate points, which are chosen to be the new landmarks if they bear a profile most similar to the mean profile for that point (obtained during training). In order to identify this point, the typical similarity measure used in most Active Shape Model (ASM) implementations is the minimum Mahalanobis distance of the candidate profile from the mean profile. Standard ASMs search for candidate points only in a one-dimensional region around a landmark. However, they searched in a bi-dimensional region 5×5 -sized around a landmark at all levels of the image pyramid [76]. Later, they analyzed the role of individual face shape and texture features in the same field. They independently investigated approaches to combine the information obtained from every component to improve face verification performance. A set of 79 landmark were manually annotated on each face. In order to quantify how much a query facial shape differs from the global mean shape, all shape vectors are aligned adopting Procrustes analysis. This step is necessary in order to discard all rotation, scale, and translation traces. Once all shape vectors are aligned, a global mean shape is built and a shape variation covariance matrix is computed. Then, Mahalanobis measures between each shape and the global mean are computed. The average distance between probe face and the global mean shapes is determined using all images of that person and will thus represents the class shape. People with a single facial feature which deviates significantly from the global mean of that feature are isolated. Given that the Mahalanobis metric is scale-invariant and basically quantify the similarity between query and mean, the distance is always expected to be valued less than 0.5 to indicate a low deviation from the mean and over 1.5 to indicate a high deviation. Using this observation, they were able to isolate individuals who deviated from the global mean shape when all 79 landmarks are taken into consideration. “People whose class shapes are far from the global mean shape have at least one visible feature of facial geometry that puts them apart from the crowd. This makes shape-based recognition a feasible technique” [77].

Cai, Wang, and Xu presented a new image distance for KFDA for face recognition and compared the results with canonical similarity distances, such as the Mahalanobis distance [24]. Ober, Neugebauer, and Sallee explored the feasibility of biometric identification adopting multiple one-dimensional human body measurements for both bi-dimensional and three-dimensional data. They also used Euclidean distance and normalized Euclidean distance for the similarity score. The Mahalanobis distance was used to calculate the similarity score [63].

There are two other types of Mahalanobis measures: Mahalanobis angle and Mahalanobis cosine measure. The **Mahalanobis angle** is defined this way:

$$D_{Mahalanobis\_Angle}\left(x_i, x_j\right) = \arccos \frac{\sum_{k=1}^{d} x_{ik}^{T} \Sigma^{-1} x_{jk}}{D_{Euclidean}\left(0, x_i\right) D_{Euclidean}\left(0, x_j\right)}, \tag{3.4}$$

where, Σ is the covariance matrix. For images, u and v with corresponding projections m and n in Mahalanobis space, the **Mahalanobis cosine measure** is [74]:

$$D_{MahCo\sin e}(u, v) = -\cos(\theta_{mn}) = -\frac{|m||n|\cos(\theta_{mn})}{|m||n|} = -\frac{m \cdot n}{|m||n|} \tag{3.5}$$

Katadound provided insight into different methods available for face recognition and explored methods that provided an efficient and feasible solution. He explained few of the most commonly used distance measures in face recognition, including Mahalanobis cosine distance, Mahalanobis L_1 and Mahalanobis L_2 [74].

Chang, Bowyer, and Flynn addressed multimodal 2D+3D face recognition. PCA-based approaches were tested separately for different modes, while match scores for various facial spaces were combined for multimodal recognition. The Mahalanobis cosine metric was adopted in the matching process [71].

McCool aimed to improve face recognition by examining two issues. The first is to examine feature distribution modelling as an improved method for verifying to feature vectors; rather than using distance- or angular-based similarity measures. The second is to examine methods for performing classifier score fusion to improve face recognition; of particular interest is multimodal fusion. Several similarity measures were tested to improve the accuracy of the eigenfaces technique. Among them, Mahalanobis distance, angular Mahalanobis measure and Mahalanobis cosine (MahCosine) are taken into consideration [78].

Amberg, Knothe, and Vetter described an emotion-invariant approach "by fitting an identity/expression separated three-dimensional Morphable Model to shape data". The fitting is achieved with robust non-rigid Iterative Closest Point (ICP) method. Similarity between faces is measured as the angle between the face parameters in Mahalanobis space, as the authors observed that the angular measure gives slightly larger recognition rates than the Mahalanobis distance. The Mahalanobis angle has the effect of regarding all caricatures of a face, which lie on a ray from the origin towards any identity, as the same identity. They also evaluated other measures, but found them to be consistently worse than the Mahalanobis angle [79].

PERFORMANCES

Mahalanobis distance reached high recognition rates in PCA face recognition method. Generally, it was compared to taxicab and Euclidean distances, cosine similarity measure, and angle.

Draper, Yambor, and Beveridge processed a combination of classic similarity distances (**taxicab**, **Euclidean**, **angle**, **Mahalanobis**) in eigenspace to enhance performance during matching phase. Mahalanobis distance, when adopted alone, was statistically significant compared to the other three alone, and no combination of these distances appears to perform better than Mahalanobis alone. In particular, six pairwise comparisons were performed between the four distances. As an outcome, the only differences are between Mahalanobis and the others. A traditional PCA classifier performed better when Mahalanobis distance is adopted rather than taxicab, Euclidean, or angle. "Mahalanobis was again superior when 60% of the eigenvectors were used. However, when only the first 20 eigenvectors were used, Euclidean, angle and Mahalanobis were equivalent". L_1 performed slightly worse. The simulations undertaken with more measures altogether did not bring any meaningful performance enhancement. Furthermore, the correlation between Manhattan, Euclidean, angle, Mahalanobis, and their shared bias, suggests that, although enhancements could be achieved by combining Manhattan distance with other distances, such enhancements are likely to be insubstantial. Mahalanobis metric is not used for Gabor wavelet representation, as "it involves transformed data and covariance matrix" more tailored to PCA-based scenarios [10].

Liu and Wechsler tested **Euclidean distance**, **taxicab distance**, **Mahalanobis distance**, and **cosine similarity measure**. They carried out a comparative performance of well known face recognition approaches such as Gabor wavelet, PCA, Fisherfaces, EFM, combination of Gabor and PCA, and combination of Gabor and Fisherfaces. Concerning PCA, Mahalanobis distance performed more efficiently than taxicab, followed in order by the L_2 and cosine similarity measure [14-16]. The reason of its superior performance is that Mahalanobis counteracts the fact that Manhattan and Euclidean distances in the eigenface space preferentially weighted low frequencies. This is consistent with the outcomes gained by Moghaddam and Pentland [80] and Sung and Poggio [81]. "The superiority of the cosine similarity measure to the others can be revealed only when the discriminating features, derived by the GFC method, rather than the expressive features [typical of PCA] are used for classification", in which this distance performed the worst among all the measures, as it "does not compensate the low frequency preference" [15]. The experimental results suggest that Mahalanobis distance measure should mainly and transversally be adopted.

Chang, Bowyer, and Flynn used **Mahalanobis cosine distance** for the matching process in a PCA-based face recognition. Mahalanobis cosine distance metric significantly outperformed L_1 and L_2, for both bi-dimensional and three-dimensional face recognition [71].

Shi, Samal and Marx evaluated the performance of four similarity measures for complex PCA: **Euclidean**, **taxicab**, **Mahalanobis**, and **eigenvalue-weighted cosine** (EWC). Generally, EWC and Mahalanobis distances are better than taxicab and Euclidean; L_2 clearly is the worst performer, consistently with results reported previously. The reason is that Manhattan and Euclidean distances "give equal weights to both high and low frequency eigenratios", thereby flattening the importance of features. EWC and Mahalanobis distance, however, weight eigenratios with their eigenvalues. In particular, EWC is at comparable to, and in some cases better than, Mahalanobis, but worse than the refined Procrustes distance. Also, the two best similarity measures are adopted to analyse the effects of emotion and aging, and for which they performed slightly worse than the refined Procrustes distance. In regard to direct face recognition, if Mahalanobis or EWC distance is adopted, "the performances are the same as the upper bound identification performance of partially automatic algorithms". One-to-one face verification is slightly worse than the refined Procrustes distance. Nonetheless, the ratio-based face model combined with either Mahalanobis or EWC could be used reliably for direct face verification of frontal faces affected by either emotion or aging [37].

Lower results were obtained by Yampolskiy and Govindaraju [38] and Izmailov and Krzyżak [44], who showed that Mahalanobis distance was slightly inferior to Euclidean and Manhattan distances.

Table **2** shows numerical results.

Table 2: Features of Mahalanobis distance

Similarity Measure	Metric	Algorithms	Face Data Type	Dimension	Reliability (Recognition Rate)	Sensitivity to Noise	Computational Cost	References
Mahalanobis Distance	Yes	PCA		2D	80%	Medium	Medium	Liu and Wechsler [14-16]
					42% (Percent of Images Correctly Recognized)			Draper, Yambor and Beveridge in 2002 [10]
		Improved PCA		2D	85.9%			Izmailov and Krzyżak in 2009 [44]
		PCA		2D	0.79 (Cumulative Match Score)			Shi, Samal and Marx in 2006 [37]

CHAPTER 4

Hausdorff Distance for Face Recognition

Abstract: When two sets are differently sized, the Hausdorff distance can be computed between them, even if the cardinality of one set is infinite. Different versions of this distance have been proposed and employed for face verification, among which the modified Hausdorff distance is the most famous. The important point to be noted is that, among the most commonly used similarity measures, the Hausdorff distance is the only one that has been widely applied to 3D data.

Keywords: Hausdorff distance, directed Hausdorff distance, partial Hausdorff distance, modified Hausdorff distance, doubly modified Hausdoff distance, weighted Hausdorff distance.

PREVIOUS WORK

"In many applications such as stereo matching not all points from an input set have a corresponding point in the output set. The two point sets may be differently sized, so that no one-to-one correspondence exists between all point pairs. In this case, a typical dissimilarity measure is the Hausdorff distance. The Hausdorff distance is defined also for unlimited point sets, in particular on nonempty closed bounded subsets of any metric space" [7].

The **Directed Hausdorff Distance** (DHD) $D_{DHD}(A,B)$ is defined as the lowest upper bound, *i.e.* the *supremum*, over all points in A of the distances to B:

$$D_{DHD}\left(A,B\right)=\sup_{a\in A}\inf_{b\in B} D_{Euclidean}\left(a,b\right). \tag{4.1}$$

The (undirected) **Hausdorff distance** is the maximum of $D_{DHD}(A,B)$ and $D_{DHD}(B,A)$:

$$D_{Hausdorff}\left(A,B\right)=\max\left\{D_{DHD}\left(A,B\right),D_{DHD}\left(B,A\right)\right\}. \tag{4.2}$$

It is shown in Fig. (**5**).

The Hausdorff distance is very sensitive to noise; a single outlier can significantly affect its value. For finite point sets, a less sensitive connected measure is the **Partial Hausdorff Distance** (PHD), introduced in 1992. It is the maximum of the two **Directed Partial Hausdorff Distances** (DPHD):

Enrico Vezzetti and Federica Marcolin

$$D_{PHD,k}\left(A,B\right)=\max\left\{D_{DPHD,k}\left(A,B\right),D_{DPHD,k}\left(B,A\right)\right\}, \tag{4.3}$$

"where, the directed distances are defined as the kth value in increasing order of the distance from a point in *A* to *B*":

$$D_{DPHD,k}\left(A,B\right)=k^{th}\inf_{a\in A\ b\in B} D_{Euclidean}\left(a,b\right). \tag{4.4}$$

The partial Hausdorff distance is not a metric, as it fails the triangle inequality [7].

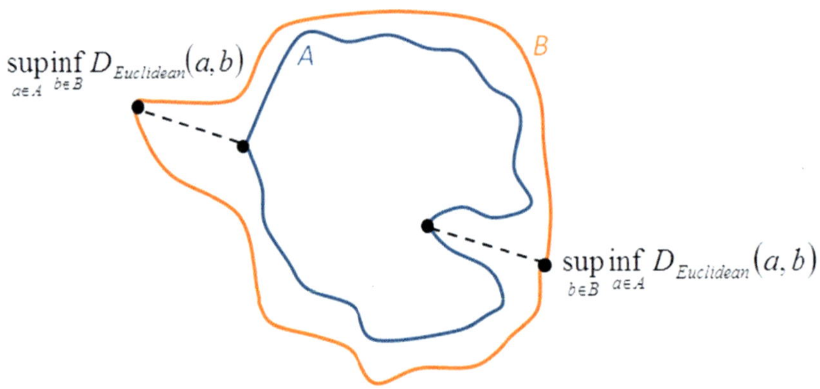

Figure 5: Components of the calculation of the Hausdorff distance between the blue line *A* and the orange line *B*.

For finite point sets, the partial Hausdorff distance is not as sensitive as the standard form of Hausdorff distance, but it is not a metric. Alternatively, the Hausdorff distance of $A,B\subseteq X$, X having a finite number of elements, can be written as:

$$D_{Hausdorff}\left(A,B\right)=\sup_{x\in X}\left|D_{Euclidean}\left(x,A\right)-D_{Euclidean}\left(x,B\right)\right|. \tag{4.5}$$

The *supremum* is then replaced by an average:

$$D_{MHD,p}\left(A,B\right)=\left(\frac{1}{|X|}\sum_{x\in X}\left|D_{Euclidean}\left(x,A\right)-D_{Euclidean}\left(x,B\right)\right|^{p}\right)^{1/p}, \tag{4.6}$$

where, $D_{Euclidean}(x,A)=\inf_{a\in A} D_{Euclidean}(x,a)$, resulting in the pth **order mean Hausdorff distance**. $|X|$ is the cardinality of set *X*, namely the number of its elements. This is less sensitive to noise, but still not robust enough [7]. The

Modified Hausdorff Distance (MHD), introduced in 1994 for comparing noise-affected synthetic images, is defined this way:

$$D_{MHD}\left(A,B\right)=\frac{1}{|A|}\sum_{a\in A}D_{Euclidean}\left(a,B\right). \tag{4.7}$$

If an image is divided into different parts, the contribution of these parts to image matching may differ. The **Weighted Hausdorff Distance** (WHD)

$$D_{WHD}\left(A,B\right)=\frac{1}{|A|}\sum_{a\in A}w(a)D_{Euclidean}\left(a,B\right), \tag{4.8}$$

where,

$$\sum_{a\in A}w(a)=|A|, \tag{4.9}$$

introduced in 2001, is the right choice. It is the most suitable for face recognition. The **Censored Hausdorff Distance** (CHD), introduced in 1997 for comparing binary images, is

$$D_{CHD,pq}\left(A,B\right)=\underset{a\in A}{p^{th}}\,\underset{b\in B}{q^{th}}\,D_{Euclidean}\left(a,b\right), \tag{4.10}$$

while the **Least Trimmed Square Hausdorff Distance** (LTS-HD), introduced in 1999, is defined as:

$$D_{LTS-HD}\left(A,B\right)=\frac{1}{H}\sum_{i=1}^{|A|}D_{Euclidean}\left(a,B\right)_{(i)}, \tag{4.11}$$

where, H denotes $h\times|A|$ and $D_{Euclidean}\left(a,B\right)_{(i)}$ represents the ith distance value in the sorted sequence $\left(D_{Euclidean}\left(a,B\right)_{(1)}\le D_{Euclidean}\left(a,B\right)_{(2)}\le\ldots\le D_{Euclidean}\left(a,B\right)_{(|A|)}\right)$. "The measure $D_{LTS-HD}\left(A,B\right)$ is minimized by keeping distance values after large distance values are removed. Thus, even if the object is occluded or damaged by noise, this matching scheme yields accurate results" [5]. An optimal fraction $h\in[0,1]$ depends on the occlusion amount. If h is equal to 1, this Hausdorff distance corresponds to the conventional MHD [5, 82, 83]. HD was originally thought and adopted for point sets on planes, *i.e.* in the bi-dimensional framework.

However, the previous equations could be applied to data points on 3D space as well [84].

In many fields, the Hausdorff distance in all its forms is considered one of the best similarity measures, although it is not a metric. It is also largely employed in many face recognition applications.

Huttenlocher, Klanderman, and Rucklidge dealt with object recognition. They investigated complex domains by matching dense oriented edge pixels. View translation, rotation, scaling are adopted to approximate complete 3D motion. HD quantifies matches between a query image and an object model [85, 86].

Takács introduced a face comparison and facial databases screening method. The proposed shape matching approach works “on edge maps and derives holistic similarity measures”. In particular, they proposed as face similarity measure a variation to the Hausdorff distance, the **“doubly” Modified Hausdorff Distance** (M2HD), by introducing the notion of a neighbourhood function (N) and associated penalties (P):

$$D_{M2HD}\left(a,B\right)=\max\left(I\min_{b\in N_B^a}\left\|a-b\right\|,(1-I)P\right), \qquad (4.12)$$

where, N_B^a is a neighbourhood of point a in set B. I is an indicator which equals 1 if there exist a point $b\in N_B^a$; equals 0 otherwise. The proposed M2HD is suitable to frameworks where shape similarity is kept constant and where the matching process undergoes small non-rigid local distortions [87].

Achermann and Bunke proposed a range image analysis application to face recognition. After a standard facial position is stated, they obtained “two different representations of the range data, based on point sets and voxel arrays, respectively”. For recognition, a three-dimensional version of the partial HD was introduced. The Hausdorff distance between each image in the test set and in the model set is calculated, so that the query image is classified according to the lowest value of the HD. It is a benefit of the HD that no problem-specific knowledge is requested to compare two sets [84].

Jesorsky, Kirchberg, and Frischholz presented a shape comparison method for face detection that could be robust to illumination and background variations. The approach is edge-based and works on grey-scale still images. HD is adopted as similarity distance between a general facial model and possible instances of the object within the image [88].

Gao and Leung proposed a new line segment HD. They extended the employment of Hausdorff distance as similarity measure to match two sets of line segments. The method incorporates structural and spatial information to quantify similarity, even in human face context. The proposed **Line segment Hausdorff Distance** (LHD) is then adopted to match objects:

$$D_{LHD}(A,B) = \max\{D_{DLHD}(A,B), D_{DLHD}(B,A)\}, \tag{4.13}$$

where, $D_{DLHD}(A,B)$ is the directed LHD:

$$D_{DLHD}(A,B) = \frac{1}{\sum_{a_i \in A} l_{a_i}} \sum_{a_i \in A} l_{a_i} \cdot \min_{b_j \in B} D_{Euclidean}(a_i, b_j). \tag{4.14}$$

A and *B* are two finite line segment sets, l_{a_i} is the length of line segment a_i [89]. Then, Gao proposed an approach for HD-based "face matching and screening". This approach adopts dominant points instead of edge maps as features for evaluating similarity. A new form of HD was conceptualized for matching. MHD was further modified and used to match significance-based dominant point rather than binary pixels, which required more storage than dominant points. A **new Modified Hausdorff Distance** (M^2HD) was introduced by embedding the merit value of each dominant point into the computation of the HD. It is defined as

$$D_{M^2HD}(A,B) = \max\{D_{DM^2HD}(A,B), D_{DM^2HD}(B,A)\}, \tag{4.15}$$

where,

$$D_{DM^2HD}(A,B) = \frac{1}{\sum_{a \in A} W_{a,b}} \sum_{a \in A} W_{a,b} \cdot \min_{b \in B} \|a - b\|. \tag{4.16}$$

$W_{a,b} = \frac{1}{2}(W_a + W_b)$ is the average merit of dominant point *a* and *b*. W_a and W_b are merits provided by an algorithm presented by Gao, not treated here [90].

Lee and Shim proposed a face recognition method based on Depth-Weighted Hausdorff Distance (DWHD) adopting curvatures. The approach also incorporates depth information of local features of the face. They also evaluated the performance of several Hausdorff distance measures [91].

Baudrier, Millon, Nicolier, and Ruan introduced an adaptative local dissimilarity distance for one-to-one comparison among images. A local Hausdorff distance is defined. Let A and B be two bounded sets of points of $\Re^2$, and W a convex closed subset of $\Re^2$. The **windowed Hausdorff distance** is [92, 93]

$$D_{Windowed\_HD}(A,B) = \max\left\{D_{D\_Windowed\_HD}(A,B), D_{D\_Windowed\_HD}(B,A)\right\}, \quad (4.17)$$

where,

$$D_{D\_Windowed\_HD}(A,B) = \max_{a \in A \cap W}\left\{\min\left\{\max_{b \in B \cap W} d(a,b), \max_{w \in Fr(W)} d(a,b)\right\}\right\} \quad (4.18)$$

Russ, Koch, and Little presented a three-dimensional face recognition method relying on HD. The typical three-dimensional formulation of the Hausdorff matching approach was enhanced to work on a bi-dimensional range image, with computation reduction and no large storage requirements. Two local Hausdorff distances are adopted "to enable fine tuning of initial facial data registration, reduce the time associated with finding the minimum error between points, and determine discriminators" for face verification task. The two measures they considered are the **Local Neighbourhood Hausdorff Fraction** (LNHF) and the **Mean Squared Error Constrained Hausdorff Distance** (MSEHD) defined as follows:

$$D_{LNHF}(A,B) = \frac{\sum_{a \in A} w_D\left(d_{N^a}(a,B)\right)}{P},$$
$$D_{MSEHD,N^a}(A,B) = \frac{\sum_{a \in A} w_D\left(d_{N^a}(a,B)\right) d_{N^a}(a,B)}{\sum_{a \in A} w_D\left(d_{N^a}(a,B)\right)}, \quad (4.19)$$

where, $d_{N^a}(a,B) = \min_{b \in N_B^a} \|a-b\|$ and $w_D(x)$ is equal to 1 for $x \leq D$ or 0 otherwise. LNHF provides a similarity quantification between two datasets. "For instance, the ratio of points in set *B* within distance *D* of the points in *A* is computed". While MSEHD indicates the quality of the fit and is significant only if the Hausdorff fraction is meaningful [94].

In their works, Kakadiaris and his co-authors [95, 96] worked on silhouetted face profiles. They explored "feature space of profiles under various rotations with a three-dimensional face model". Two different profile identification methods were compared: the first one based on matching three-dimensional and bi-dimensional profiles represented explicitly adopting MHD; the second adopting a hierarchy of SVM classifiers "applied on rotation-, translation-, and scale-invariant features extracted from profiles".

PERFORMANCES

Generally, Hausdorff distance was not compared with other distance metrics. It is due to its different structure and definition. Nevertheless, its recognition rate is to be considered. It was employed especially in matching algorithms with 3D data.

Gao compared face images adopting **Hausdorff distance**-based face matching. In particular, he computed the identification accuracy of MHD, PHD, and M^2HD for edge maps and dominant points. With dominant points, MHD verification rate (top one identification) was 93.34% "due to the use of less feature points and dominant point extraction errors". Performance improved with M^2HD by integrating the importance value of each dominant point, which correctly identified 94.17% (top one identification). In top one identification, the correct match is only counted when the best matched face from gallery set is exactly the face of the same person of the query image. In the top *N* screening, the correct match is counted when the "right" input face is among the best *N* matched faces from library. "The accuracy of M^2HD matching on dominant points was slightly lower than that of MHD matching on edge maps. M^2HD on dominant points correctly identified all the test images using top 13 screening, while MHD on edge maps correctly identified them using top 10 screening". The screening result of M^2HD on dominant points increased by 2.7%. Nonetheless, computational time and storage space of M^2HD on dominant points were reduced to 3.7% and 19.3% compared to those of MHD on edge maps, respectively. "By using dominant points, MHD performed worse than MHD on edge maps". Screening/identification results were also obtained for the PHD adopting median

NN distance on edge maps and dominant points, respectively. The result was that MHD was outperformed by PHD with median NN distance [90].

A lower result was obtained by Wang, Zhang, and Feng [54]. Image Euclidean distance outperformed Hausdorff distance.

Table **3** summarizes the performances.

Table 3: Features of various Hausdorff distances

Similarity Measure	Metric	Algorithms	Face Data Type	Dimension	Reliability (Recognition Rate)	Sensitivity to Noise	Computational Cost	References
Modified Hausdorff Distance (MHD)	no	Matching	Dominant Points	3D	93.34%	High		Gao in 2003 [90]
			Edge Maps		95.84%			
		NN	Dominant Points		85%			
			Edge Maps		88%			
Doubly Modified Hausdorff Distance (M^2HD)	no	Matching	Dominant Points		94.17%		3.4% of Time Required for MHD	
		NN	Dominant Points		86%			
Partial Hausdorff Distance (PHD)	no	NN	Dominant Points		92%			
			Edge Maps		93%			

CHAPTER 5

Cosine-Based Distances, Correlations, and Angles for Face Recognition

Abstract: The cosine distance compares the feature vectors of two images by returning the cosine of the angle between two vectors. Other cosine- and angle-based measures are here presented, including Tanimoto dissimilarity and Jaccard index, together with other correlations; they have been employed in algorithms relying on PCA, ICA, NN, and Gabor wavelets, especially on bi-dimensional facial data. Only correlation coefficients have been applied on three-dimensional point clouds.

Keywords: Angle distance, cosine distance, cosine similarity measure, Pearson correlation, Tanimoto dissimilarity, Jaccard index.

PREVIOUS WORK

Classification techniques that are based on angular methods have been studied by a number of researchers. The most direct approach is to use **angular separation**, or **angle distance**, between feature vectors as a distance pseudo-metric. This is defined as

$$D_{Ang}\left(x_i,x_j\right)=\arccos\frac{x_i\cdot x_j}{\|x_i\|\|x_j\|}=\theta\left(x_i,x_j\right),$$

where, $\theta\left(x_i,x_j\right)$ is the angle between the vectors x_i and x_j, and is taken to be in the range $\left[0,\pi\right]$. A closely related pseudo-metric is the **cosine distance**

$$D_{\cos}\left(x_i,x_j\right)=1-\frac{x_i\cdot x_j}{\|x_i\|\|x_j\|}=1-\cos\theta\left(x_i,x_j\right), \tag{5.1}$$

where, $D_{\cos}\left(x_i,x_j\right)$ lies in the range $\left[0,2\right]$ [8]. The cosine distance compares the feature vectors of two images and computes the cosine of the angle between two vectors [97].

When cosine distance is converted into a similarity measure in the range $\left[-1,1\right]$, with a value of 1 indicating maximum similarity, it is referred to as the **Normalised Correlation** (NC) or **cosine similarity measure** and is defined as,

Enrico Vezzetti and Federica Marcolin

$$D_{cosine\_similarity\_measure}\left(x_i, x_j\right) = \frac{x_i \cdot x_j}{\left\|x_i\right\|\left\|x_j\right\|} = 1 - D_{\cos}\left(x_i, x_j\right). \tag{5.2}$$

When applying these angular measures, it is assumed that the data is first centred by subtracting the training set mean vector [8]. The cosine similarity is widely used for clustering directional data, which only measures the relative direction between pairs of unit vectors. This distance is the natural distortion measure for prototype-based clustering, under the assumption that the data were generated by a mixture of von-Mises Fisher distributions. This similarity has also been applied to the field of information retrieval including text analysis, bioinformatics and collaborative filtering. The **weighted** (or parametrized) **cosine similarity** is a generalization of the cosine similarity in which a positive-definite matrix A is used:

$$D_{weighted\_cosine}\left(x_i, x_j\right) = \frac{x_i A x_j}{\left\|x_i\right\|_A \cdot \left\|x_j\right\|_A}, \tag{5.3}$$

where, $\|x\|_A$ is the weighted L_2-norm: $\|x\|_A = \sqrt{x^T A x}$ [4]. It has also been shown that the **Pearson correlation** is a form of cosine similarity:

$$D_{Pearson\_correlation}\left(x_i, x_M\right) = \frac{\sum_{k=1}^{N}\left(x_{ik} - Mx_i\right)\left(x_{Mk} - Mx_M\right)}{\sqrt{\left(x_{ik} - Mx_i\right)^2} \cdot \sqrt{\left(x_{Mk} - Mx_M\right)^2}}, \tag{5.4}$$

where, x_i is the input pattern vector, x_M is the mean pattern vector, and

$$Mx_i = \frac{1}{N}\sum_{k=1}^{N} x_{ik}, \tag{5.5}$$

$$Mx_M = \frac{1}{N}\sum_{k=1}^{N} x_{Mk}. \tag{5.6}$$

The Pearson correlation coefficient was chosen as an alternative similarity measure based on the statistical relation between the two vectors.

For PCA-based nearest neighbour face recognition algorithms, the **whitened cosine distance** is commonly used. For example, this is the baseline algorithm chosen for performance comparison on the FRGC experiment set. The whitened cosine measure is similar to cosine distance but with an additional whitening transformation being first applied to ensure that the training set has unit variance in all directions. This is accomplished by pre-multiplying x_1 and x_2 in equation (5.1) by $\Lambda^{-1/2}U^T$ where, $U\Lambda U^T = S$ is the eigen-decomposition of the sample covariance matrix *S*. Other two whitened cosine similarity measures are the probability reasoning model whitened cosine and the within-class whitened cosine. The **Probability Reasoning Model Whitened Cosine** (PWC) similarity measure replaces Λ in the whitening transformation by a diagonal matrix whose i^{th} entry is the mean of the individual class variances in the ith direction; in FRGC experiments it yields slightly better results than the standard whitened cosine measure. The **Within-Class Whitened Cosine** (WWC) similarity measure uses the mean within-class scatter matrix in place of the total scatter matrix *S* and achieves substantially better results on FRGC experiments. Lastly, the **weighted angle similarity measure** is defined as

$$D_{WA}\left(x_i, x_j\right) = \sum_{k=1}^{N} \frac{w_k x_{ik} x_{jk}}{\|x_i\|\|x_j\|}, \tag{5.7}$$

where, the weighting factors w_k are given by $\sqrt{1/\lambda_k}$ with λ_k being the variance in the ith direction. The whitened cosine distance performs reasonably well, however recognition accuracy is shown to degrade as the number of PCA features increases [8].

The cosine-based similarity measures were widely used for face recognition, especially the cosine similarity measure.

O'Toole, Cheng, Phillips, Ross, and Wild assessed the adequacy of computational algorithms as models of human face processing. The algorithms were all based on PCA and varied only in the similarity measures. Cosine distance was one of them [28].

Liu and Wechsler introduced GFC for face recognition. The set of similarity measures adopted to evaluate the efficiency of different representation and recognition methods included the cosine similarity measure [14-16].

Wu, Yoshida, and Shioyama described a face identification method with Gabor filters. Facial organ regions are detected with colour and edge information, followed by corner detection in each detected facial organ region. For each small image region around a point, they estimated the similarity between the small region of the query image and the corresponding region of each face of the gallery with a normal correlation method [98]. Jiao, Gao, Chen, Cui, and Shan adopted local feature analysis. Gabor jets on feature points and their spatial distances represented the face. Some metrics are used, including angular separation [30].

Katadound provided insight to different methods available for face recognition, and explore methods that provided an efficient and feasible solution. The cosine distance is used as a distance measure between the probe image and the images stored in the database as a decision parameter to determine the best match [74]. Ebrahimpour introduced fractal methods. Differences between images are captured in non-geometrical or luminance parameters. Cosine distance appears among the employed similarity measures [31]. Later, he presented and ensemble based techniques for face recognition. The distance between two features is measured with some distances including cosine similarity measure [32].

Yang, Gao, Zhang, and Yang formulated ICA in the kernel-inducing feature space and developed a two-phase kernel ICA algorithm: KPCA plus ICA. A NN classifier with different distance metrics is adopted for classification. Cosine distance is used both in PCA and KPCA methods, and in ICA and KICA, as this metric was demonstrated most effective for ICA [34]. Zhang, Shan, Zhang, Gao, and Chen introduced Multi-Resolution Histograms of Local Variation Patterns (MHLVP), where facial images are represented by the concatenation of the spatial histogram of local variation patterns computed from the multi-resolution Gabor features. In their experiment, the normalized correlation is used as a similarity measure in LDA and correlation algorithm to compare feature vectors [99]. Trias evaluated well-known face verification approaches, such as PCA, ICA and LDA, on classical databases. The **correlation metric**, similar to normalized correlation, together with other distances, is used as a measure of similarity and dissimilarity [67]:

$$D_{CORR}\left(x_i, x_j\right) = \frac{\sum_k \left(x_{ik} - \hat{x}_i\right)\left(x_{jk} - \hat{x}_j\right)}{\sqrt{\sum_k \left(x_{ik} - \hat{x}_i\right)^2 \sum_k \left(x_{jk} - \hat{x}_j\right)^2}}. \tag{5.8}$$

Perlibakas adopted PCA and Log-Gabor filters. For recognition, cosine-based distance measure is used [100]. Smith, Kittler, Hamouz, and Illingworth examined an extension of LDA, called angular LDA, where a non-linear transformation is applied after LDA representation. An ensemble of SVM classifiers operating in the angular LDA space resulted to be more accurate than the same classifiers operating in the classic LDA space. Given that the Euclidean metric is not the optimal metric to adopt with LDA, the cosine similarity measure is used. The best classification accuracy is obtained by using the angle between two vectors as a dissimilarity measure. This is the basis of the NC classification technique, in which the cosine of the angle between a query vector and class mean vector is used as a measure of similarity [21]. Shi, Samal and Marx investigated the role of landmarks in PCA face recognition. They analyzed the effectiveness of three similarity distances including cosine similarity measure. They also defined a new similarity measure called the **Eigenvalue-Weighted Cosine** (EWC) distance:

$$D_{EWC}\left(x_i, x_j\right) = -\sum_{k=1}^{N} \frac{\dfrac{x_{ik} x_{jk}}{\lambda_k^2}}{\sqrt{\sum_{k=1}^{N}\left(\dfrac{x_{ik}}{\lambda_k}\right)^2 \sum_{k=1}^{N}\left(\dfrac{x_{jk}}{\lambda_k}\right)^2}}, \qquad (5.9)$$

where, λ_k are the eigenvalues of the covariance matrix [37].

McCool examined the fusion of a bi- and three-dimensional face verification systems, the so-called multimodal classifier score fusion. These verification systems compare two feature vectors, *i.e.* image representations, using distance- or angular-based similarity distances. The cosine similarity measure is taken into consideration [78]. Graves and Nagarajah proposed a modified monotonic function model for multi-class classification applications in biometric recognition. Many similarity measures are adopted to quantify the "degree-of-similarity" between each input pattern vector and a particular class. The functions were linearly proportional to the cosine distance and other similarity distances. To measure the degree of similarity, functions proportional to many similarity measures were employed. Among them, the Pearson correlation coefficient was used [40].

Ionita focused on a face modelling approach to face recognition. In particular, 2D modelling techniques known as Active Appearance Models (AAM) are studied. A number of improvements on the standard AAM formulation are given, which can be separated into two main approaches. A directional lighting-enhanced AAM is proposed, by integrating a dedicated illumination subspace. Making full use of colour image information is another major approach, where model enhancements which yield increased accuracy are demonstrated. These enhanced models are integrated into a model-based, automatic, face recognition algorithm, where they are shown to have a direct, positive impact on the overall recognition rates. The cosine similarity measure was used as a measure for feature classification [101].

Sadeghi, Samiei, and Kittler dealt with fusing PCA-based and LDA-based similarity measures for face verification. They investigated a variety of metrics, including NC and correlation coefficient-based distance [2, 22].

Delac, Grgic, and Grgic investigated JPEG and JPEG2000 for face recognition. As a distance metric they adopted the cosine angle for ICA [35].

The cosine similarity metric may be extended to the Jaccard coefficient in the case of binary attributes. This is the Tanimoto coefficient. Arodź used Radon transform properties for face recognition. The **Tanimoto similarity measure** is used for comparison. This measure exactly coincides with the **Jaccard index**, also known as **Jaccard similarity coefficient**. It is a statistic used for comparing similarity and dissimilarity of sample sets. The Jaccard coefficient is defined as the size of the intersection divided by the size of the union of the sample sets A and B:

$$D_{Jaccard}(A,B)=\frac{|A\cap B|}{|A\cup B|}. \tag{5.10}$$

In mathematical form, if samples X_i and X_j are bitmaps, X_{ik} is the kth bit of X_i , then the Tanimoto similarity ratio is

$$D_{Tanimoto}(X_i,X_j)=\frac{\sum_k (X_{ik}\wedge X_{jk})}{\sum_k (X_{ik}\vee X_{jk})}. \tag{5.11}$$

If each sample is modelled as an attribute set, this value is equal to the Jaccard coefficient of the two sets. If the Tanimoto similarity is expressed over a bit vector, it can be written as

$$D_{Jaccard}(x_i,x_j)=D_{Tanimoto}(x_i,x_j)=\frac{x_i\cdot x_j}{|x_i|^2+|x_j|^2-x_i\cdot x_j}, \tag{5.12}$$

which is expressed in terms of vector scalar product and magnitude. For a bit vector, where the value of each dimension is 0 or 1, then

$$x_i \cdot x_j = \sum_k \left(x_{ik} \wedge x_{jk} \right) \quad (5.13)$$

and,

$$|x_i|^2 = \sum_k \left(x_{ik} \right). \quad (5.14)$$

It is important to note that the Tanimoto similarity measure is equal to the Jaccard similarity coefficient, but the Tanimoto distance differs from the Jaccard distance. These distances have two different expressions that are not used in this work [33].

Other similarity measures based on correlations have been adopted in the context of face recognition. Classical **correlation coefficient** was adopted as similarity measure between probe and gallery images by Ibrahim, Guan, and Niazi for a new filtering method [102]. Kim, Ju, So, and Kim introduced **Directional Local Correlations** (DLC) to measure intensity similarity between a local region and each of the counterparts for local texture feature-based face recognition. DLC is a sort of correlation coefficient whose absolution is less than or equal to unity [103]. Li, Shan, Chen, and Gao have recently adopted **canonical correlations**. They addressed the issue 'how to measure the possibility whether two non-corresponding face regions belong to the same face.' This possibility is measured *via* canonical correlation, which solves the problem of selecting basis vectors for two sets of variables in such a way that the correlation between the projections of the variables onto these basis vectors are mutually maximized [104]. Canonical correlation was also adopted by Chu, Chen, and Lien. The group introduced **canonical difference**, a geometric perspective of canonical correlation, to measure similarity between pairs of subspaces in a KPCA-based new algorithm called Kernel Discriminant Transformation working on image sets [105].

PERFORMANCES

Although cosine-/angle-based distances and correlations were widely used for PCA, their performances showed the best rates for ICA method. Here only good results are reported.

Liu and Wechsler used **Euclidean distance**, **taxicab distance**, and **cosine similarity measure**. As already reported, results showed that under the cosine similarity measures the Gabor features carried more significant information than PCA features do. When PCA is tested, Mahalanobis distance was compared to these measures. It achieved the best percentage. While for PCA method, Mahalanobis distance rates exceed cosine ones [14-16].

Arodź used the Radon transform properties to help face recognition with the nearest neighbour decision rule. Several metrics for transformed images were evaluated, including **Euclidean** and **Manhattan** distance and the **Tanimoto** dissimilarity measure. The Tanimoto and Euclidean metrics gave better recognition accuracy than the Manhattan metric [33].

Yang, Gao, Zhang, and Yang employed PCA, KPCA, ICA, and KICA for face feature extraction. One-hundred features are extracted to describe facial images. A NN classifier with different distance metrics is adopted for classification. **Euclidean**, **taxicab**, and **cosine distance** are used in PCA and KPCA. Only cosine distance is adopted in ICA and KICA, as this measure was demonstrated to be most effective for ICA [34].

Shi, Samal and Marx evaluated the performance of four similarity measures for complex PCA: **Euclidean distance**, **taxicab distance**, **Mahalanobis distance**, and **EWC.** The EWC distance and the Mahalanobis distance are in general superior to the popular L_1 and L_2. As previously summed up, the ratio-based face model combined with either the Mahalanobis or the EWC distance provided accurate face matches and effectively reduced face image search space, even for frontal view faces that are complicated by either expression or aging. In general, the EWC distance is at par with, and in some case superior to, the Mahalanobis distance, but worse than the refined Procrustes distance [37].

Although recognition rates are not so low, especially for improved versions of angle- and cosine-based similarity measure, some works proved that other measures outperformed them. Draper, Yambor, and Beveridge [10], Benedikt and the co-authors [106, 107], Graves and Nagarajah [40], Sadeghi, Samiei, and Kittler [2, 22] showed that Mahalanobis distance, Weighted hybrid derivative DTW (WDTW), Euclidean, and GD rates were superior to those of angular separation, correlation coefficients, cosine distance metric and Pearson correlation coefficient, and normalized correlation, respectively.

Table **4** summarizes the rates.

Table 4: Features of cosine- and angle-based similarity measures

Similarity Measure	Metric	Algorithms	Face Data Type	Dimension	Reliability (Recognition Rate)	Sensitivity to Noise	Computational Cost	References
Cosine Similarity Measure	No	PCA		2D	38%	medium	medium	Liu and Wechsler [14-16]
		PCA + NN		2D	60.5%			Yang, Gao, Zhang, and Yang in 2005 [34]
		KPCA + NN		2D	60.5%			
		PCA + LDA		2D	94.4%			Graves and Nagarajah in 2007 [40]
		LDA		2D	TEE = 15.24; TET = 19.79			Sadeghi, Samiei, and Kittler [2, 22]
		Independent Component Analysis (ICA) + NN		2D	70%			Yang, Gao, Zhang, and Yang in 2005 [34]
		kernel ICA (KICA) + NN		2D	73.75%			
		Gabor Wavelets		2D	72%			Liu and Wechsler [14-16]
Eigen-Weighted Cosine Distance	No	PCA		2D	0.8 (Cumulative Match Score)			Shi, Samal and Marx in 2006 [37]
Angle	Pseudo-Metric	PCA		2D	34% (Percent of Images Correctly Recognized)			Draper, Yambor and Beveridge in 2002 [10]
Pearson Correlation Coefficient	No	PCA + LDA		2D	94.4%			Graves and Nagarajah in 2007 [40]
		LDA		2D	TEE = 16.17; TET = 21.90			Sadeghi, Samiei, and Kittler [2, 22]
Correlation Coefficients	No	Matching	Point Cloud	3D	Quantified by a Graph			Benedikt and the co-authors [106, 107]
Tanimoto Dissimilarity	No	PCA	images	2D	81%			Arodź in 2004 [33]
		PCA w/o First 3 Components			89%			
		Fisherfaces Method			94%			
		Radon Transform Properties-Based Method (With No Side-Illuminated Images) + NN			96%			
		Radon Transform Properties-Based Method + NN			89%			

CHAPTER 6

Other Distances for Face Recognition

Abstract: Other distances are employed for face recognition, but their usage within the field is less preponderant than the previous ones. This chapter collects these measures, which are known as bottleneck, Procrustes, Earth mover's, and Bhattacharyya distances. A subsection dealing with performances is only presented for the Bhattacharyya distance, which, although a non-extensive application in the field of face recognition, is one of the most efficient measures of the branch.

Keywords: Bottleneck distance, Procrustes distance, Earth mover's distance, transport distance, Bhattacharyya distance.

BOTTLENECK DISTANCE

The disadvantage of Hausdorff distance is in mapping, that is defined as an association of points from *A* to its nearest neighbour in *B*. It does not always have to be a one-to-one mapping. In the case where this correspondence is needed, *i.e.*, where each point from *A* is just matched by only one point from *B*, there is better to use the **bottleneck distance**. It is defined as:

> *let A and B be two point sets of size N and* $d(a,b)$ *a distance between two points. The bottleneck distance* $D_{bottleneck}$ *is the minimum of the maximum distance* $d(a,f(a))$ *over all one-to-one mapping f between A and B [6].*

For calculating the distance $d(a,b)$ between two points, a traditional L_p distance can be chosen. "An alternative is to compute an approximation $\tilde{D}_{bottleneck}$ to the real bottleneck distance $D_{bottleneck}$. An approximate matching between *A* and *B* with the furthest matched pair, such that $D_{bottleneck} < \tilde{D}_{bottleneck} < (1+\varepsilon) D_{bottleneck}$, can be computed. Variations to the bottleneck distance are the minimum weight distance, the most uniform distance, and the minimum deviation distance" [7].

The bottleneck distance was employed for shape comparison, less frequently in face recognition field.

Baudrier, Millon, Nicolier, and Ruan presented a method for binary image comparison. The bottleneck distance, minimum weight matching, uniform matching, and minimum deviation matching are cited as similarity measures for image comparison [92, 93].

Enrico Vezzetti and Federica Marcolin

Cohen-Steiner, Edelsbrunner, and Harer dealt with comparing and classifying geometric shapes. The bottleneck distance was used to measure the distances between persistence diagrams and resulted valuable for this approach [68].

Chazal, Cohen-Steiner, Guibas, Mémoli, and Oudot introduced a family of signatures for finite metric spaces endowed with functions based on persistence diagrams. They proved the stability of their signatures under Gromov-Hausdorff space perturbations. They also extended these outcomes "to metric spaces equipped with measures". Their signatures are tailored to unstructured point cloud data, such as faces, which they illustrated through a shape classification application. Calculating the Gromov-Hausdorff distance between two finite metric spaces seems unfeasible in most of the cases. To distinguish such spaces from a metric point of view, it is thus important to exhibit reasonable lower bounds with controlled computation. The results showed that the bottleneck distances computed among persistence diagrams of finite metric spaces are reasonably bounded [108].

PROCRUSTES DISTANCE

There are many versions of the **Procrustes distance** form. The first one is given by Dryden and Mardia [109, 110]. They discussed shape models and described their role in high-level image analysis. They also described an application in Bayesian image analysis for landmarking on facial images adopting a scale-space model. The Procrustes (Riemannian) shape distance is used as a measure for shape analysis between two landmark configurations :

$$D_{Procrustes}\left(f_1, f_2\right) = \arccos \frac{\sum_j \left(l_{1j} - \overline{f}_1\right)^* \left(l_{2j} - \overline{f}_2\right)}{\left(\sum_j \left(l_{1j} - \overline{f}_1\right)^2 \sum_j \left(l_{2j} - \overline{f}_2\right)^2\right)^{1/2}}, \tag{6.1}$$

where, the notation is similar to that of the previous *formula* and the asterisk stands for the complex conjugate [109, 110].

Shi, Samal and Marx studied landmark exploitation for face recognition with bi-dimensional regression. "For two object superimposition, the goodness-of-fit of bi-dimensional regression of the Euclidean transform is measured by the Procrustes distance", defined as:

$$D_{Procrustes}(f_1, f_2) = \inf_{\beta,\theta} \frac{J(\beta,\theta)}{\left\| f_1 - \overline{f_2} \right\|_2^2} = \frac{\left| f_1^H f_1 - \frac{f_1^H f_2 f_2^H f_1}{f_2^H f_2} \right|}{\left\| f_1 - \overline{f_1} \right\|_2^2}. \tag{6.2}$$

f is a face that is modelled by a N-dimensional vector of landmarks l_j: $f = (l_1, l_2, ..., l_N)^T$, with $l_j = x_j + iy_j$,where, (x_j, y_j) are the coordinates of l_j and $i = \sqrt{-1}$. So f_1 and f_2 represent two faces. β and θ are two numbers corresponding to scaling and rotation in the Euclidean transform; $\overline{f_1} = \frac{1}{N}\sum_{j=1}^{N} l_j$ and H denotes the Hermitian transpose. A refined Procrustes distance, equal to the one in (6.1) is then employed as a similarity measure [37, 75].

Clemmensen, Gomez, and Ersbøll identified significant facial features in elastic net model selection for facial verification. Modelling the features that are crucial for person discrimination *via* the adoption of features subsets has the double action of decreasing computational cost and increasing potentiality of the facial verification algorithm. "The elastic net model is able to select a subset of features with low computational effort compared to other feature selection methods". The performance of the approach is compared with geometry- and colour-based methods widely adopted in facial verification such as Procrustes NN. Given two configurations of facial landmarks x_j and x_k, the Procrustes distance between them is defined by

$$D_{Procrustes}(x_j, x_k) = \inf_{\beta,\theta,a,b} \left\| \frac{x_k}{\|x_k\|} - \frac{x_j}{\|x_j\|} \beta \cdot e^{i\theta} - a - ib \right\|, \tag{6.3}$$

where, $i = \sqrt{-1}$, $\|\cdot\|$ represents the $L_2 - norm$, and the parameters β, θ, a, and b, which denote scaling, rotation, and translation of configuration x_j, are chosen to minimize the distance between x_j and x_k. They also proposed a refined PCA-based Procrustes distance. The configurations, namely the key face representations, are first centred at the origin and then unit-sized. Afterward, a complex PCA is carried out to reduce dimensionality. The similarity distance is defined in this lower m-dimensional space by

$$D_{R\_Procrustes}\left(x_j, x_k\right) = \sum_{k=1}^{m} \left\| \frac{\hat{x}_k}{\sqrt{\lambda_k^{(z)}}} - \frac{\hat{x}_j}{\sqrt{\lambda_k^{(w)}}} \right\|, \tag{6.4}$$

where, $\hat{x}_k$ is the kth eigenvector of configuration x_k, $\hat{x}_j$ is the kth eigenvector of configuration x_j, and $\lambda_k^{(z)}$ and $\lambda_k^{(w)}$ the corresponding eigenvalues [111].

Chellappa and Turaga's group reviewed some recent advances in video-based face recognition scenario. Particularly, they summarized the uses and advantages of videos in improving accuracy of the tasks related to still data, *i.e.* recognition or localization. "The squared Procrustes distance for two points x_i, x_j on the Grassmann manifold is computed using orthonormal basis X_i and X_j of the respective subspaces as the smallest squared Euclidean distance between any pair of matrices in the corresponding equivalence classes". The Grassmann manifold $G_{k,m-k}$ is the space whose points are *k*-planes and *k*-dimensional hyperplanes (containing the origin) in $\Re^m$. Hence:

$$D_{Procrustes}\left(x_i, x_j\right) = \min_R tr\left(X_i - X_j R\right)^T \left(X_i - X_j R\right), \tag{6.5}$$

where, *R* is a $k \times k$ full rank real matrix. When *R* varies over all $k \times k$ real matrices, the Procrustes distance is given by

$$D_{Procrustes}\left(x_i, x_j\right) = tr\left(I_k - A^T A\right), \tag{6.6}$$

where, $A = X_i^T X_j$ and I_k is a $k \times k$ identity matrix [112, 113].

Perakis, Theoharis, Passalis, and Kakadiaris introduced a three-dimensional landmarking approach that processes facial databases with pose rotations of up to 80° around the *y*-axis. Thus, the so automatically-extracted landmarks are adopted to robustly select face zones from three-dimensional datasets of faces. Alignment is gained *via* minimization of the Procrustes distance

$$D_{Procrustes}\left(x_i, x_M\right) = \sum \left|x_i - x_M\right|^2, \tag{6.7}$$

of each shape x_i to the mean x_M. This alignment analysis is widely called Procrustes Analysis and is adopted to evaluate mean landmark shape [114].

The definition of Rara, Elhabian, Ali, Miller, Starr, and Farag is similar. They introduced a face recognition framework with dense and sparse stereo reconstruction. The adopted Procrustes distance between two shapes x_i and x_j is the sum of squared point distances:

$$D^2_{Procrustes}\left(x_i, x_j\right) = \left\|x_i - x_j\right\|^2. \tag{6.8}$$

"There is no dimensional change with rigid alignment by adopting Procrustes; similar shapes are have a minor Procrustes distance after rigid alignment and geometric information of faces (*e.g.*, distance ratios between face parts) are maintained" [115-117]. Performances of the Procrustes distance are reported in Table **6**.

EARTH MOVER'S DISTANCE

The **Earth Mover's Distance** (EMD) is a type of distance function based on the minimal amount of work required to transport the earth or mass from one position to the other. As a matter of fact, it is also called **transport distance**. For example, when it is necessary to quantify the distance between two distributions *via* Earth mover's distance, then one distribution can be considered as an earth mass well spread in space and the other as a holes collection in the same space. The computation of the EMD is given by the minimal distance that is needed to transport the earth into the holes (a quantity of the mass of the earth and the size of the hole is represented by weight values for the given distribution). Let $d(x, y)$ be a ground distance function and $A = \{a_1, a_2, ..., a_m\}$, $B = \{b_1, b_2, ..., b_m\}$ be two weighted point sets such that $a_i = (x_i, w_i)$, $i = 1,...,m$ and $b_j = (y_j, u_j)$, $j = 1,...,n$, $x_i, y_j \in \Re^k$ with $w_i, u_j \in \Re^+ \cup \{0\}$ being its corresponding weight. Let also W and U be the total weights of set A and B, respectively:

$$W = \sum_{i=1}^{m} w_i\,,\ U = \sum_{j=1}^{m} u_j\,. \tag{6.9}$$

Denote with f_{ij} the elementary flow of the weight (of the earth) from x_i to y_j, over the elementary distance $d(x_i, y_j)$, then a set of all feasible flows $F = [f_{ij}]$ is defined by the following constraints:

- $f_{ij} \geq 0, \qquad i = 1,...,m, \qquad j = 1,...,n$

- $\sum_{j=1}^{n} f_{ij} \le w_i, \quad i = 1,...,m$

- $\sum_{i=1}^{m} f_{ij} \le u_j, \quad j = 1,...,n$

- $\sum_{i=1}^{m}\sum_{j=1}^{n} f_{ij} = \min(W,U)$

$\mathrm{EMD}(A,B)$ is defined as "the minimum total cost over all possible $\overline{F}$ normalized by the weight of the lighter set":

$$D_{EMD}(A,B) = \frac{\min_{F \in \overline{F}} \sum_{i=1}^{m}\sum_{j=1}^{n} f_{ij} d_{ij}}{\min(W,U)}. \tag{6.10}$$

Generally, that distance function does not obey the conditions of the positivity and the triangle inequality, and it is very computationally expensive. For all that, some nice properties are satisfied when some additional conditions are held [6].

The EMD is a discrete version of the so-called Monge-Kantorovich distance, but is known with other different names. Monge first defined it in 1781 "to describe the most efficient way to transport piles of soil. It is called the Augean Stable by David Mumford, after the story in Greek mythology about Hercules's dirt piles moving from the huge cattle stables of king Augeas. The name here and most widely used is coined by Jorge Stolfi. It has been applied to heat transform problems, object contour matching, and colour-based image retrieval" [7].

The Earth mover's distance is quite used for face recognition applications. Surong, Liang-Tien, and Rajan proposed a new approach to quantify similarity between images by adopting dominant colour descriptor. With EMD, good retrieval results are gained compared with those gained with the traditional MPEG-7 reference software (XM). To further enhance accuracy, texture information from edge histogram descriptor is added. To reduce computational time, two methods, *i.e.* lower bound of EMD and M-tree index based on EMD distance, are investigated "which can prune the images far from the query image". MPEG-7 visual descriptors form a multi-coloured collection of image and video features including colour, texture, shape, and motion of visual content [118, 119].

Li, Wang, and Tan presented a Earth mover's distance-based facial verification method for video frames. Well-known approaches could be classified into sequential approach, by computing a similarity function among videos, and batch approach, by computing the angle between subspaces or finding Kullback-Leibler (KL) divergence between probabilistic models. The proposed approach is more straightforward. They introduced a metric, adopted as classifier, relying on an average Euclidean distance between two videos, by adopting EMD as the underlying similarity measure among face image distributions. Dimensionality is reduced for efficiency. Fisher's LDA is used "for linear transformation and for making each class more separable. The set of features is then compressed with a signature, composed of points with their corresponding weights". In the matching phase, the dissimilarity between two signatures is evaluated through EMD [120].

Xu, Yan, and Luo investigated face recognition robust to pose variations. Firstly, they formulated an asymmetric similarity distance relying on Spatially constrained EMD (SEMD), "for which the source image is partitioned into non-overlapping local patches". The output image is given by a set of overlapping local patches at different positions. "Assuming that faces are roughly aligned according to eye position, one patch in the input image can be matched only to one of its neighbouring patches in the output image under the spatial constraint of reasonably small misalignments". Given that the SEMD-based similarity distance is asymmetric, they proposed two methods for combining the two similarity distances calculated in the two directions. Furthermore, they adopted a "distance-as-feature approach by treating the distances to the reference images as features in a Kernel Discriminant Analysis (KDA) framework" [121].

Zhou, Ahrary, and Kamata presented the Local Quaternion Patters (LQP) to represent the feature parts of the face. In order to maintain facial spatial feature, the asymmetric similarity measure Weighted Spatially constrained EMD (WSEMD) is investigated for classification purpose. "The source image is partitioned into non-overlapping local patches". The output image is given by a collection of "overlapping local patches at different positions". Gaussian Kernel is adopted. Finally, local and global weights are applied to enhance the performance of the classifier [122].

BHATTACHARYYA DISTANCE

The **Bhattacharyya distance** is a statistic measure for quantifying the similarity between two discrete or continuous probability distributions. It is named after

Anil Kumar Bhattacharya, a 1930s statistician of the Indian Statistical Institute. If p and q are two discrete probability distributions over the same domain X, the Bhattacharyya distance between them is give by:

$$D_{Bhattacharyya}\left(p,q\right)=\sum_{x}\sqrt{p(x)q(x)}\;,\; x\in X\,. \tag{6.11}$$

It was quite used in face recognition. Huet provided a hierarchical framework of object recognition methods from large structural libraries. The Bhattacharyya distance was considered as a similarity measure between line patterns [9].

Sim and Zhang investigated face recognition by exploring facial image space. They first synthesized images with various conditions of lighting and position, then estimated the probability density function (pdf) for every person. Thus, the pdfs are analysed in terms of separability and overlap. Class regions, where the Bayes's classifier classifies each person, are also stated and undergone to k-means clustering. By taking into exam cluster boundaries and centres, they determined the most discriminating lighting/pose conditions and viewing conditions for face recognition. They showed that the typical inter-class/intra-class variability is not an accurate dissimilarity distance between two pdf classes, and instead proposed the adoption of Bhattacharyya. The Bhattacharyya distance is a more robust separability measure, while the inter-class/intra-class ratio depends on variability direction, thus is not as dependable [123].

Arandjelović and Cipolla recognized faces from video sequences in a realistic unconstrained framework where lighting, pose, and user motion patterns have a wide variability and facial images are of low resolution. Bhattacharyya distance was taken into consideration among the similarity measures [50, 51].

Manikarnika suggested an algorithm which could detect faces in a general setting and which could operate in real time. The algorithm uses a colour segmentation in order to locate suitable regions which are then merged together to give a collection of candidate regions. The candidate regions are then analysed using a wavelet strategy. For fast processing the Haar wavelet was used. Features are extracted from the wavelet coefficients by using a set of simple statistical measurements. Candidate regions are accepted or rejected as a face by calculating the Bhattacharya between the feature vectors [124].

Bernardin, Stiefelhagen, and Waibel presented a tracking and identification method "in a smart environment using distantly-located audio-visual sensors". The method relies on the embedding of tracking and face/voice identification cues, obtained *via* several cameras and microphones. A probabilistic model is adopted to constantly track of the verified subjects and to keep up-to-date the belief in their identities with new observations. The Bhattacharyya distance is adopted as similarity distance among discrete pdfs [125].

Paliy, Sachenko, Kurylyak, Boumbarov, and Sokolov described a face detection combined approach for grey-scale images with neural network classifiers, which consist of "Haar-like feature cascade of weak classifiers and convolutional neural network". It produced excellent detection rates on CMU test set and the processing speed resulted consistent with video flows timings. Lastly, they extracted meaningful face features for pose estimation and verification. Adopting the Bhattacharyya distance, they compared the similarity between the grey-scale coefficients over the detected face x_i and those of the mean face x_M :

$$D_{Bhattacharyya}\left(x_i, x_M\right) = \sum_j \sum_k \sqrt{T_i\left(j,k\right) T_M\left(j,k\right)}. \tag{6.12}$$

In the context of face detection, this similarity measure seems unsuitable for concrete applications, as it heavily slows down the global performance [126].

Yao, Wang, Lin, and Chai presented an Incremental Bhattacharyya Dissimilarity (IBD) for evaluating histogram-based descriptors in particle weight estimation algorithms. "IBD is defined by incorporating an Incremental Similarity Matrix (ISM) into the Battacharyya dissimilarity. Such an ISM enables a cross-bin interaction during the comparison between matched bin patches of two input histograms", thus improving discriminating capability between the object and background particles. They proposed a robust method for computing ISM by adopting spatiotemporal attributes, leading to an effective tracking process. Experimentations show that IBD has dependable discriminative potential compared to other state-of-the-art dissimilarity distances [72].

PERFORMANCES

Bhattacharyya distance is particularly known for its low computational cost and low sensitivity to noise. Performances are to be considered, especially in its in incremental form. It was used in PCA method, pairwise histogram comparison and particle filtering. For its computational cost and the rates, it is considered one of the most effective similarity measures.

Huet compared **taxicab** and **Euclidean** distance measures, **Bhattacharyya**, **Matusita** distance and **divergence** for object recognition. The Bhattacharyya distance measure, the Matusita distance and the divergence are able to perform noticeably better that the standard L_1 and L_2. The sensitivity study accessing the retrieval performance of the different distances under varying quality of segmentation revealed that the Bhattacharyya and Matusita distance measures are robust to significant differences in the segmentation process (extra and missing segments). Indeed, both distance measures outperform the divergence measure in many situations. As expected, the Matusita distance produces identical indexing results than the Bhattacharyya. However, they favoured the use of the Bhattacharyya distance measure for computational reasons [9].

Sim and Zhang measured separability of face pdfs by adopting both **Bhattacharyya** and **inter-class/intra-class ratio**. Bhattacharyya distance gives a more reliable separability measure, while the inter-class/intra-class is not reliable enough [123].

Yao, Wang, Lin, and Chai evaluated their **IBD** and eight other dissimilarity distances, including χ^2 **statistic dissimilarity**, L_2 **distance**, **KSD**, **KL divergence**, **EMD-**L_1, **DD**, **QD**, and standard **Bhattacharyya** "on a well collected dataset", for discriminative capability in particle filtering algorithms. Since χ^2 statistical dissimilarity, L_2 distance, and KL also rely on "bin-to-bin comparison nature", the related outcomes are close to that of Bhattacharyya. In regard to KSD and EMD-L_1, "they cannot output stable observation likelihood surfaces, as their matching properties are not sufficient for measuring particles" (PF). Given that QD is not learnt from a well collected sample set, its performance is low. Among the comparative dissimilarity distances, DD shows relatively better accuracy, due to its multi-scale comparisons. However, experimental results showed that incremented Bhattacharyya had dependable discriminative capability and its algorithm based on PF demonstrates an acceptable performance in overcoming hardships related to partial occlusion and background cluster, compared to other state-of-the-art distances [72].

Table **5** shows the numerical results.

Table 5: Features of Bhattacharyya distance

Similarity Measure	Metric	Algorithms	Face Data Type	Dimension	Reliability (Recognition Rate)	Sensitivity to Noise	Computational Cost	References
Bhattacharyya Distance (BD)	No	Pairwise Histogram Comparison	Histograms	2D	76.5%	low	low	Huet in 1999 [9]
		PCA + Pairwise pdf Comparison	Cloud + pdfs	3D + 2D	Good - Quantified by a Graph			Sim and Zhang in 2004 [123]
Incremental Bhattacharyya (IBD)	No	Particle Filtering (PF)	Histogram-Based Descriptors	2D	Good - Quantified by a Graph			Yao, Wang, Lin, and Chai in 2010 [72]

CHAPTER 7

Errors for Face Recognition

Abstract: Distances between faces may also be seen as errors. Error types are various and may differ depending on the application, but have been used for face recognition. The main outcomes have been collected and are reported in this brief but key chapter.

Keywords: Sum square error, mean square error, average point to point error, me17, me4.

PREVIOUS WORK

Perlibakas compared fourteen distances and their modified versions among feature vectors with respect to the performance of PCA method, by also proposing a modified Sum Square Error (SSE)-based distance

$$D_{MSSE}\left(x_i,x_j\right)=\frac{\sum_k\left(x_{ik}-x_{jk}\right)^2}{\sum_k x_{ik}^2\sum_k x_{jk}^2}, \tag{7.1}$$

and the weighted modified SSE-based distance

$$D_{WMSSE}\left(x_i,x_j\right)=\frac{\sum_k w_k\left(x_{ik}-x_{jk}\right)^2}{\sum_k x_{ik}^2\sum_k x_{jk}^2}, \tag{7.2}$$

where, x_i and x_j are two eigenfeature vectors, $k=1,\dots,n$, and $w_k=\frac{1}{\lambda_k}$. They also used classical SSE and Mean Square Error (MSE) [17]:

$$D_{SSE}\left(x_i,x_j\right)=\sum_k\left(x_{ik}-x_{jk}\right)^2, \tag{7.3}$$

$$D_{MSE}\left(x_i,x_j\right)=\frac{1}{n}\sum_k\left(x_{ik}-x_{jk}\right)^2 \tag{7.4}$$

Cristinacce, Cootes, and Scott described a shape constraint technique to be inserted in a multi-phase feature localization method. The coarse-to-fine approach

Enrico Vezzetti and Federica Marcolin

firstly applies a face detector to retrieve approximate facial image scale and location. Then, individual feature detectors are applied and combined adopting the new Pairwise Reinforcement of Feature Responses (PRFR) algorithm. The obtained points are then refined using a version of AAM tuned to edges and corners. “To assess the accuracy of feature detection, the predicted feature locations are compared with manually annotated points”. The **average point to point error** (me) is calculated as follows:

$$D_{me} = \frac{1}{ns}\sum_{i=1}^{n} d_i , \tag{7.5}$$

where, d_i are the point to point errors for each individual feature location and s is the known inter-ocular distance between left and right eye pupils. Here n is the number of modelled points. The search error “me” computed over 17 detected face features is called **me17**. When it is computed for the eye pupils and mouth corners only, it is referred to as **me4** [127]. Then, they presented a model matching approach adopting a joint shape and texture appearance model, similar to AAM, to build up a collection of region template detectors. “The model is fitted to an unseen image in an iterative manner by generating templates using the joint model and the current parameter estimates, correlating the gallery images with the query to generate response images and optimising the shape parameters” for maximizing the sum of responses. They kept “me” as a distance measure for comparison [128]. Lastly, they fitted a set of local feature models to an image within the ASM setup. Two different non-linear boosted feature models, a conventional feature detector classifier and a boosted regression predictor, trained with GentleBoost were compared. The “me” distance is used to compute the distance between computed landmarks and those manually labelled [129].

Beumer, Tao, Bazen, and Veldhuis explored and compared two face landmarking approaches for the purpose of face recognition: the Most Likely-Landmark Locator (MLLL), based on likelihood ratio maximization, and Viola-Jones detection. Both adopt locations of eyes, nose, mouth, and other facial features as landmarks. Moreover, they proposed “a landmark-correction method (BILBO) relying on projection into a subspace”. The mean localization errors and their effects on recognition accuracy are quantified. Given that the images in the databases are variously scaled, they calculated the Root Mean Square (RMS) error of the remaining difference between the found shape and the ground truth shape. This is in the form of percentage of the inter-ocular distance [130]. Senaratne and Halgamuge adopted “landmark model matching” consisting of four steps:

"creation of the landmark distribution model, face finding, landmark finding, and recognition". They suggested an approach to quantify the performance of face finding phase. The eyes midpoint stands as the approximate representation for face detection. They compared the error between the actual midpoint and the estimated one. Given that the face sizes significantly differed between each other, the error ε was normalized with the distance between left and right eye, as [57].

$$\varepsilon = \frac{\left\| \vec{x}_{true} - \vec{x}_{est} \right\|}{\left\| \vec{x}_{lefteye} - \vec{x}_{righteye} \right\|} \times 100\% \tag{7.6}$$

CHAPTER 8

Similarity Functions for Face Recognition

Abstract: Similarity functions are not distances, but functions aimed to evaluate the similarity between two objects. Some of them relate to some other previously explained measures, such as cosine distance. Others are statistical or probabilistic, or rely on fuzzy logic. It has not been possible to provide a comprehensive table with recognition rates, as the data were to different to be compared.

Keywords: Similarity function, dissimilarity function, kernel function, Tversky's similarity function.

PREVIOUS WORK

Similarity functions are not distances, but functions used to compute the similarity between two objects. They are widely used for many applications, also including face recognition, in various forms.

Lades, Vorbruggen, Buhmann, Lange, von der Malsburg, Wurtz, and Konen presented an object verification method from video frames based on dynamic link architecture, *i.e.* an extension to classical artificial neural networks. "Memorized objects are represented by sparse graphs, whose vertices and edges are labelled by a multi-resolution description in terms of a local power spectrum" and geometrical distance vectors, respectively. Elastic graph matching is here carried out *via* stochastic optimization of a matching cost function. For jets J^I and J^M in image and model domain, respectively, the similarity function employed for vertexes is defined as

$$S_v\left(J^M, J^I\right) = \frac{J^I \cdot J^M}{\left\|J^I\right\|\left\|J^M\right\|}. \tag{8.1}$$

The form is equal to that of cosine similarity measure, given in (5.2). Being invariant to variations in jet length, S_v was robust to lighting variations. The edge labels of both image and model graphs are compared though a quadratic comparison function

$$S_e\left(\vec{\Delta}_{ij}^I, \vec{\Delta}_{ij}^M\right) = \left(\vec{\Delta}_{ij}^I - \vec{\Delta}_{ij}^M\right)^2, \tag{8.2}$$

Enrico Vezzetti and Federica Marcolin

where, $\vec{\Delta}_{ij} = \vec{x}_j - \vec{x}_i$ is the Euclidean distance between two vertices [131].

Wiskott *et al.* worked on Gabor wavelet transform *via* elastic graph matching. For an image graph G with nodes $n = 1,...,N$ and edges $e = 1,...,E$ and an Face Bunch Graph (FBG) B with model graphs $m = 1,...,M$, a new similarity function is defined as

$$S_B(G,B) = \frac{1}{N}\sum_n \max_m \left(S_\varphi\left(J_n^I, J_n^{Bm}\right)\right) - \frac{\lambda}{E}\sum_e \frac{\left(\Delta\vec{x}_e^I - \Delta\vec{x}_e^B\right)}{\left(\Delta\vec{x}_e^B\right)^2}, \tag{8.3}$$

where, λ concerns "the relative importance of jet similarities and the topography term". J_n are the jets at node n and $\Delta\vec{x}_e^B$ are the distance vectors adopted as labels at edges e. "FBG provides several jets for every key point. The best fitting jets serve as the local experts for the image face". A heuristic algorithm selects the image graph that maximizes the graph similarity function [132, 133]. Then, Wiskott compared two elastic graph matching algorithms. The adopted similarity function is given by

$$S\left(G^M, G^I\right) = \max_{d_1 d_2} \frac{1}{N_M} \sum_{m_1 m_2} \max_{p_1 p_2} S_a\left(\zeta^M_{m_1 m_2}, \zeta^I_{(m_1+d_1+p_1)(m_2+d_2+p_2)}\right), \tag{8.4}$$

where, G^M and G^I are model and image graph, respectively. $S_a\left(\zeta^M, \zeta^I\right)$ indicates the similarity between model and image jets, without taking into account phase information [134].

Chung, Kee, and Kim developed a two-phase approach based on PCA and Gabor filter responses. The first part concerns Gabor filtering on predefined key points "that could represent features from the original face image". The second part deals with conversion of these face features into eigenspace *via* PCA. Hence, the trained facial model "has some eigenvalues that can be derived from ensemble matrix of given Gabor responses". To perform face identification, "test images are also projected into eigenspace and compared to the trained facial images in the same eigenspace". To compare the similarity of the values in the eigenspace, the similarity function (8.1, below) is used. With PCA, L_2 norm was adopted to quantify similarity, but the similarity function (8.1) is more effective in eigenspace [135].

Duc, Fischer, and Bigun applied elastic graph matching to facial identity check. The traditional matching error was not strong enough to provide satisfying results.

So, they introduced an automatic weighting of the nodes according to their importance. The distance between two graphs is assessed by a dissimilarity function that takes into consideration both the feature vectors of each node and the deformation information attached to the edges. They investigated dissimilarity measures where the contribution from nodes and edges were independent, more precisely

$$d\left(G^1,G^2\right)=\sum_{i=1}^{N_v} d_v\left(G_{v_1}^1,G_{v_1}^2\right)+\lambda\sum_{j=1}^{N_e} d_e\left(G_{e_j}^1,G_{e_j}^2\right), \tag{8.5}$$

where, $G_{v_1}^1$ represents the ith node of grid G^1, $G_{e_j}^2$ is the ith node of grid G^2, N_v and N_e are the node and edge number, respectively, and λ is a weight representing graph stiffness [136].

Liao and Li dealt with multiple facial features. Each feature is formalized through a Gabor complex vector and is located *via* facial feature detection method. Two different similarity functions are adopted for different purposes. The first is phase-insensitive and mainly used for feature discrimination:

$$S\left(x_i,x_j\right)=\frac{\sum_k x_{ik}x_{jk}}{\sqrt{\sum_k x_{ik}^2\sum_k x_{jk}^2}}, \tag{8.6}$$

where, x_i and x_j represent the facial features. The second is phase-sensitive and plays a core role in locating features:

$$S_p\left(x_i,x_j\right)=\frac{\sum_k x_{ik}x_{jk}\cos\left(\phi_{ik}-\phi_{jk}-\vec{d}\vec{w}_k\right)}{\sqrt{\sum_k x_{ik}^2\sum_k x_{jk}^2}}, \tag{8.7}$$

where, ϕ_k is the phase of each component of vector, $\vec{w}_k$ is the characteristic wave vector of the respective Gabor filter, and $\vec{d}$ is an estimated displacement that "compensates for the rapid phase shifts" [137].

Wang, Chua, and Ho presented a feature-based facial verification approach relying on three-dimensional range data and bi-dimensional grey-scale facial images. "Feature points are described by Gabor filter responses in the 2D domain and point signature in the 3D domain". The extrapolated shape and texture features are firstly projected into their own subspace adopting PCA. "In subspace, the corresponding normalized shape and texture weight vectors are then merged to form an augmented vector representing each facial image. For a given probe facial image, the best match in the face gallery is identified according to similarity function or SVM". They used (8.1) as similarity measure to compare shape and texture information. All the similarities between a query image and all images from model library are computed relying on this measure. It is similar to that of the cosine similarity measure. The best-matched face is the one with the highest value of similarity with the probe facial image [138].

Escobar and Ruiz-del-Solar proposed a face recognition system that uses LogPolar Images and Gabor Filters. This system models the way in which face images are processed between the retina and the areas of the visual system. To compare the Gabor jets of an input image with the existing ones in the face database, a similarity function equal to (8.1) is adopted. Then, to compare all the jets J^1 of an image G^1 with all the jets J^2 of another image G^2, the following expression is used [139]:

$$S\left(G^1,G^2\right)=\frac{1}{N}\sum_{k=1}^{N}S_a\left(J_k^1,J_k^2\right) \tag{8.8}$$

Kepenekci, Boray Tek, and Akar presented a feature-based approach to frontal face recognition with Gabor wavelets. The points are extracted using the local features of every face in order to reduce the effect of occlusion. To find the similarity of a probe image to library, a predefined graph is matched and jets are compared in means of a similarity function while deforming the graph. The used similarity function between two complex valued feature vectors is similar to the form (8.1), but with the absolute value on each x factor [140].

Some of these similarity functions are probabilistic, often give by the Bayes rule. Moghaddam and Pentland's group [141-145] proposed an approach for "direct visual matching" of images for verification and image retrieval. A probabilistic measure of similarity based on Bayesian (MAP) analysis of image differences is adopted:

$$S\left(I_1,I_2\right)=\frac{P\left(\Delta\mid\Omega_I\right)P\left(\Omega_I\right)}{P\left(\Delta\mid\Omega_I\right)P\left(\Omega_I\right)+P\left(\Delta\mid\Omega_E\right)P\left(\Omega_E\right)}, \tag{8.9}$$

where, I_1 and I_2 are two facial images and $\Delta = I_1 - I_2$ is an image intensity difference. Ω_I and Ω_E are two classes of facial image variations: intra-personal variations, corresponding to different facial expressions of the same individual, and extra-personal variations, between different individuals. Both classes are assumed to be Gaussian-distributed and "seek to obtain estimates of the likelihood functions $P(\Delta \mid \Omega_I)$ and $P(\Delta \mid \Omega_E)$ for a given intensity difference Δ. The priors $P(\Omega)$ can be set to specific operating conditions or other sources of *a priori* knowledge regarding the two images being matched. This particular Bayesian formulation casts the standard face recognition task (essentially an *M*-ary classification problem for *M* individuals) into a binary pattern classification problem with Ω_I and Ω_E. This problem is then solved using the maximum *a posteriori* (MAP) rule, namely two images are determined to belong to the same individual if $P(\Omega_I \mid \Delta) > P(\Omega_E \mid \Delta)$, or equivalently, if $S(I_1, I_2) > \frac{1}{2}$". An alternative probabilistic similarity measure is defined using the intra-personal likelihood alone,

$$S(I_1, I_2) = P(\Delta \mid \Omega_I), \tag{8.10}$$

thus leading to Maximum Likelihood (ML) verification as opposed to the *Maximum A Posteriori* (MAP) verification in previous form. ML is almost as effective as MAP in most cases. The same probability forms were used by Zhang, Chen, Li, and Zhang, who presented a learning technique to automate face annotation in family photograph albums. "Face annotation is formulated in a Bayesian framework, in which the face similarity distance is defined as MAP estimation". In order to manage the missing features, marginal probability is adopted so that samples with some missing features are compared with those with all features "to ensure a non-biased decision" [146]. Similarly, Wang and Tang combined Bayesian probabilistic model and Gabor filter responses for face identification to take full advantage of both methods and to boost intra-personal variation [147]. Jiao, Gao, Chen, Cui, and Shan worked on local feature analysis. The face is represented by the Gabor jets of the features and their spatial distances. The employed similarity functions are (8.1) and (8.2) [30].

Kittler, Ghaderi, Windeatt, and Matas developed a face verification method which relies on the ECOC classifier concept. They measured a between-point-similarity expressed by a **kernel function** which is maximum when the distance equals 0 and monotonically decreases as the distance increases. They adopted exponential kernels with fixed width σ. "The centres do not need to be explicitly determined, as they used $D_i(\overline{x})$ in the exponent of the kernel to measure similarity of x to class *i*. One kernel per client and a number of kernels for each imposter" were allocated. They measured the relative similarities between a probe vector and the claimed identity, and also with to the impostors as

$$k_i(\bar{x}) = \sum_{\alpha} w_\alpha \exp\left\{-\frac{d_\alpha(\bar{x})}{\sigma^2}\right\}, \tag{8.11}$$

where, index α runs over all imposter kernel placements and client *i*, and the weights w_α are estimated [11, 13]. The client claim test takes place as follows:

$$k_i(\bar{x}) = \begin{cases} \geq 0.5 & \textit{accept claim} \\ < 0.5 & \textit{reject claim.} \end{cases} \tag{8.12}$$

Santini and Jain developed a similarity measure based on **fuzzy** logic. The model is "dubbed Fuzzy Feature Contrast (FFC), an extension to a more general domain of the Feature Contrast model by Tversky". They assessed the similarity by only considering geometrical features such as mouth size and chin shape. Be *I* an image and φ_i some measurements on the image, used to assess the truth of *n* fuzzy predicates, $\mu(P(x_i)) = \mu(x_i)$. From the measurements φ_i they derived the truth values of a number *p* of fuzzy predicates and incorporated them into a vector:

$$\mu(\varphi) = \{\mu_1(\varphi), \ldots, \mu_p(\varphi)\}. \tag{8.13}$$

They called $\mu(\phi)$ the (fuzzy) set of true predicates on the measurements φ. The set is fuzzy in the sense that a predicate P_j belongs to $\mu(\varphi)$ to the extent $\mu_j(\varphi)$. They used this fuzzy set as a base to apply Tversky's theory. In order to apply the feature contrast model they calculated the fuzzy sets $\mu(\varphi) \cap \mu(\psi)$ and $\mu(\varphi) - \mu(\psi)$, and chose a tailored salience function *f*. The saliency of the fuzzy set $\mu = \{\mu_1, \ldots, \mu_p\}$ is assumed to be its cardinality:

$$f(\mu) = \sum_{i=1}^{p} \mu_i. \tag{8.14}$$

The intersection of the sets $\mu(\varphi)$ and $\mu(\varphi)$ is defined this way:

$$\mu_\cap(\phi, \psi) = \{\min\{\mu_i(\phi), \mu_i(\psi)\}\}_{i=1}^{p}, \tag{8.15}$$

while the dissimilarity between the two sets is defined as

$$\mu_{-}(\varphi,\psi)=\left\{\max\left\{\mu_i(\varphi)-\mu_i(\psi),0\right\}\right\}_{i=1}^{p}. \tag{8.16}$$

The **Tversky's similarity function** between two fuzzy sets $\mu(\varphi)$ and $\mu(\varphi)$ corresponding to measurements made on two images is given by:

$$S(\varphi,\psi)=$$
$$=\sum_{i=1}^{p}\min\left\{\mu_i(\varphi),\mu_i(\psi)\right\}-\alpha\sum_{i=1}^{p}\max\left\{\mu_i(\varphi)-\mu_i(\psi),0\right\}-\beta\sum_{i=1}^{p}\max\left\{\mu_i(\varphi)-\mu_i(\psi),0\right\} \tag{8.17}$$

It is the FFC model [148, 149]. Similarly, Widyanto proposed a fuzzy similarity measure to measure similarity between face shape representation [150].

PERFORMANCES

For their different forms, the similarity functions were not often compared to other distances. Only few results are reported in literature. Moreover, numerical recognition rates are not available.

Turaga, Veeraraghavan, and Chellappa performed the recognition experiment adopting the **Procrustes distance** and the kernel density methods. For comparison, they adopted the shape Procrustes distance and the **arc-length distance** metric. The accuracy of the techniques is compared as a noise function to signal ratio. The manifold-based approaches behaved significantly better than shape Procrustes measures. "Among the manifold methods, the kernel density method outperforms both the Procrustes and the arc-length distance measures. Given that the Grassmann manifold-based methods accurately account for the affine variations found in the shape, they outperform simple methods that do not account for affine invariance. Moreover, since the kernel methods learn a probability density function for the shapes on the Grassmann manifold, it outperforms distance-based NN classifiers using Grassmann arc-length and Grassmann Procrustes". They also computed NN classifier accuracy using Procrustes measure on Stiefel manifold [113].

CHAPTER 9

Other Measures for Face Recognition

Abstract: Other measures are employed to compute similarity between faces. Although some of them are very popular, such as edit distance or turning function distance, they may be more frequently used for object, vectors or shape comparison and less for faces. This paragraph collects all these measures and the works in which they are used for face recognition. Among them, Dynamic Time Warping (DTW), Hidden Markov Models (HMM), and Fréchet distance have been applied to 3D data.

Keywords: Dynamic Time Warping, Fréchet distance, Hidden Markov Models, arc-length distance, Histogram Intersection, Yang distance, Froboenius distance, Gradient Direction, Canberra distance.

PREVIOUS WORK

Kittler, Ghaderi, Windeatt, and Matas proposed an ECOC classifier-based method and examined an extension of LDA for face recognition. The **Hamming metric**, often used in ECOC setups, is employed as a dissimilarity measure. It collapses each x_i, namely the output vector, into a binary decision and "finds the mean number of errors when compared with the class template vector" Z_i:

$$D_{Hamming}\left(x_i, x_T\right) = \frac{1}{N}\sum_{k=1}^{N} I\left(Z_{ik}x_k < 0\right), \tag{9.1}$$

where, x_T are the target classes, $I(\cdot)$ is the indicator function, that yields either value 1 or 0 depending on whether it is applied to a true predicate or not [13, 21]. Artiklar, Hassoun, and Watta presented an input pattern shifting algorithm to improve recognition performance. They used a NN classification scheme and ranked the outputs on the basis of the Hamming distance in grey-scale images [27].

Hamza and Krim proposed a new object matching method based on geodesic distances, capable of capturing the intrinsic geometrical data structure. The is to formalize objects through a probabilistic shape descriptor which evaluates geodesic distances among pairs of points on their surfaces. In the matching phase, they calculated a dissimilarity distance among shape distributions of two arbitrary objects. "Information-theoretic measures provide quantitative entropic divergences between two probability distributions". Two traditional entropic measures are the **Kullback-**

Enrico Vezzetti and Federica Marcolin

Leibler divergence (KL, or directed) dissimilarity measure and the **Jensen-Shannon divergence** (JS), to be defined among an arbitrary number of probability distributions. Let M_1 and M_2 be two three-dimensional objects with geodesic shape distributions $\hat{p}$ and $\hat{q}$ respectively. KL divergence defined as

$$D_{KLD}\left(\hat{p},\hat{q}\right)=\int \hat{p}\left(x\right)\log_2\frac{\hat{p}\left(x\right)}{\hat{q}\left(x\right)}dx=\mathrm{E}\left\{\log\frac{p\left(x\right)}{q\left(x\right)}\right\}, \tag{9.2}$$

where, $\mathrm{E}\{\cdot\}$ denotes the expected value with respect to $p(x)$. It is non-symmetric, unbounded, and undefined if $\hat{p}$ is not absolutely continuous with respect to $\hat{q}$. To overcome these restrictions, Hamza and Krim used the JS divergence D given by

$$D_{JSD}\left(\hat{p},\hat{q}\right)=$$
$$=\frac{1}{2}\left[D_{KLD}\left(\hat{p},\frac{\hat{p}+\hat{q}}{2}\right)+D_{KLD}\left(\hat{q},\frac{\hat{p}+\hat{q}}{2}\right)\right]=H\left(\frac{\hat{p}+\hat{q}}{2}\right)-\frac{H\left(\hat{p}\right)+H\left(\hat{q}\right)}{2} \tag{9.3}$$

where, $H\left(\hat{p}\right)=-\int \hat{p}\left(x\right)\log_2\hat{p}\left(x\right)dx$ is the differential entropy, which corresponds to Shannon's entropy, "a measure of uncertainty, dispersion, and randomness", in the discrete domain. The maximum uncertainty is gained through the uniform distribution, so that the entropy could be seen as a measure of uniformity of a probability distribution. "Unlike the Kullback-Leibler divergence, the JS divergence has the strength of being symmetric, always defined, and extendable to any arbitrary number of (possibly weighted) probability distributions" [151]. Hamza and Krim applied this approach to faces. Arandjelović and Cipolla recognized faces using video sequences. The Kullback-Leibler divergence and the **resistor-average distance**, similar to the KL divergence but not asymmetric in the two distributions, are here proposed as possible dissimilarity measures between probability densities [50, 51]. Sim and Zhang proposed a way to investigate face recognition. More precisely, they estimated pdf of every person with lighting and pose changes, and measured their discriminatory potential together their inter- and intra-class ratios. They argued that the actual "measure of class separability must be computed using pdf distance metrics", such as the Kullback-Leibler divergence. Given two pdfs P_i and P_j, they also determined their **inter-class** and **intra-class distances**. "The inter-class distance measures the variability between two classes (persons), while the intra-class distance measures the variability of all the images of one person":

$$D_{inter-class}\left(P_i,P_j\right)=\left\|\mu^i-\mu^j\right\|, \tag{9.4}$$

$$D_{intra-class}\left(P_i\right)=\sqrt{\lambda_{\max}^i}, \tag{9.5}$$

where, μ^i is the mean of pdf P_i, $\lambda_{\max}^i$ is the largest eigenvalue of the covariance matrix of P_i. "Intuitively, the inter-class distance may be measured as the distance between class means" [123]. Oussalah discussed the state-of-the-art of content-based image retrieval focusing on the most significant components and reviewing different techniques adopted at each step. One of the applications is face recognition. The KL divergence distance was used as a similarity measure [152].

Ahonen, Hadid, and Pietikäinen took into consideration shape and texture information to formalize facial images. Face is firstly split up into reduced zones from which LBP histograms are extrapolated and "concatenated into a single spatially-enhanced feature histogram" representing facial image. Facial verification is achieved through a NN classifier in the computed feature space with χ^2 as dissimilarity distance. Particularly, some possible dissimilarity measures were to be applied to histograms:

- **Histogram Intersection** (HI): $D_{HI}\left(S,M\right)=\sum_i \min\left(S_i,M_i\right)$,
- **Log-likelihood statistic**: $D_{LL}\left(S,M\right)=-\sum_i S_i \log M_i$,
- **Chi square statistic**: $\chi^2\left(S,M\right)=\sum_i \frac{\left(S_i-M_i\right)^2}{S_i+M_i}$.

When the image is split up into local zones, some of these areas, such as eyes region, are expected to contain more useful discriminating information than others. To take advantage of this, weights are applied. For instance, the weighted χ^2 statistic gets the form

$$\chi_w^2\left(S,M\right)=\sum_{i,j} w_{ij}\frac{\left(S_{ij}-M_{ij}\right)^2}{S_{ij}+M_{ij}}, \tag{9.6}$$

in which w_j is the weight for region j [153]. Chen proposed a technique for extrapolating features relying on "decision level fusion of local features".

Similarly, the probe face is firstly split up into small areas from which LBP histogram sequences are extrapolated and concatenated to form a global feature representation. HI dissimilarity measure is adopted as classifier [41]. Sadeghi, Samiei, and Kittler dealt with fusing PCA-based and LDA-based similarity measures. They investigated a variety of metrics, including the chi square statistic [2, 22].

Trias evaluated well-known face verification approaches, such as PCA, ICA and LDA, on classical databases. The quadratic distance, the Canberra metric, and the nonlinear distance, together with other distances, are used as a measures of similarity and dissimilarity [67]:

- **Quadratic distance**: $D_{quadratic}\left(x_i, x_j\right) = \sqrt{\left(x_i - x_j\right)^T B\left(x_i - x_j\right)}$,
- **Canberra metric**: $D_{Camberra}\left(x_i, x_j\right) = \sum_k \frac{\left|x_{ik} - x_{jk}\right|}{x_{ik} + x_{jk}}$,
- **Nonlinear distance**: $D_{nonlinear}\left(x_i, x_j\right) = \begin{cases} 0 & if \quad D_{Euclidean}\left(x_i, x_j\right) < T \\ H & if \quad D_{Euclidean}\left(x_i, x_j\right) \geq T. \end{cases}$

The Canberra distance was also investigated by Sadeghi, Samiei, and Kittler [2, 22].

"The cumulative angle function, or **turning function**, $\Theta_A(s)$ of a polygon or polyline A computes the angle between the counter clockwise tangent and the x-axis as a function of the arc-length s. $\Theta_A(s)$ keeps track of the turning that takes place, increasing with left hand turns, decreasing with right ones. This function is invariant under polyline translation and is a piecewise-constant function, increasing or decreasing at the vertices and constant between two consecutive vertices" [7]. Having regard to the definition, this distance is not easily applicable to faces. A similar recognition field is the one regarding silhouettes. Although this book is dedicated to face, some of these parallel applications may provide ideas and advices for face recognition field. Yue and Chellappa introduced an active view synthesis method from silhouette images. After the acquisition with a virtual camera on circular trajectories of a set of virtual views of the object, they proposed a methodology for formalizing human pose from a restricted number of silhouettes. The Image-Based Visual Hull (IBVH) method is combined with a "contour-based body part segmentation" method. They derived virtual camera extrinsic parameters and synthesized the individual turntable image collection adopting the IBVH method. The adoption of the turning function distance as similarity measure between silhouettes will make this method suitable to "generate the desired pose-normalized images for recognition applications" [154, 155].

Kim and Yoon described a technique for similarity quantification between aggregated image objects. As a similarity measure, they employed the **edit distance** which had been previously largely adopted for quantifying variations among strings. The edit distance, or **Levenshtein distance**, is "the smallest number of insertions, deletions, and substitutions required to change one string or tree into another. Edit distance is used to compare character strings and applied to other domains including computer vision and molecular biology" for quantifying similarity between DNA sequences. In their case, they transformed path data sequences into string sequences representing the shapes [156].

Niennattrakul, Wanichsan, and Ratanamahatana demonstrated how multimedia data, such as videos, images, and audios, could be reduced to time series representation without any loss of significant features, to be applied to voice/face classification and recognition. They chose *k*-medoids algorithm, robust to noise and outliers, then used **Dynamic Time Warping** (DTW) measure to show the applicability of their method to cluster multimedia time series data. DTW calculates "all possible mappings between two time series data points, finding the smallest warping distance". Assume to have two time series: a sequence Q of length n, and a sequence C of length m, where,

$$\begin{aligned} Q &= q_1, q_2, \ldots, q_i, \ldots, q_n, \\ C &= c_1, c_2, \ldots, c_i, \ldots, c_m. \end{aligned} \tag{9.7}$$

First, the authors created an n-by-m matrix where every (i, j) element of the matrix is the cumulative distance of the distance at (i, j) and the minimum of the three elements neighbouring the (i, j) element, which are $(i\text{-}1, j)$, $(i, j\text{-}1)$, and $(i\text{-}1, j)$ where, $0 < i \le n$ and $0 < j \le m$. Define the (i, j) element as:

$$\begin{aligned} elem_{ij} &= d_{ij} + m_{ij}, \\ d_{ij} &= \left(q_i - c_j\right)^2, \\ m_{ij} &= \min\left\{elem_{(i-1)(j-1)}, elem_{(i-1)j}, elem_{i(j-1)}\right\}, \end{aligned} \tag{9.8}$$

where, $elem_{ij}$ is (i^{th}, j^{th}) element of the matrix, d_{ij} is the squared distance of q_i and c_j, and m_{ij} is the minimum cumulative distance of three elements surrounding the (i^{th}, j^{th}) element. Then, to select the optimal path, they chose the one with minimum cumulative distance at (*n*,*m*). The distance is defined as:

$$D_{DTW}\left(Q,C\right)=\min\left\{\sqrt{\sum_{k=1}^{K} w_k}\right\}, \tag{9.9}$$

where, w_k is (i^{th}, j^{th}) at k^{th} alignment of a warping path, and *K* is the length of the warping path [58, 157]. Benedikt and the co-authors proposed an approach to capture three-dimensional facial motions without the use of face markers. Then, they investigated behavioural biometrics pattern matching methods which operated successfully on very short facial actions. Qualitative and quantitative considerations are derived for both face detection and recognition applications. They evaluated **Fréchet distance**, DTW, Continuous DTW (CDTW), and Derivative DTW (DDTW). Let A and B be two parameterized curves $A\left(\alpha\left(t\right)\right)$ and $B\left(\beta\left(t\right)\right)$, and let their parameterizations α and β be continuous functions of the same parameter $t\in\left[0,1\right]$, such that $\alpha\left(0\right)=\beta\left(0\right)=0$, and $\alpha\left(1\right)=\beta\left(1\right)=1$. The Fréchet distance is "the minimum over all monotone increasing parameterizations $\alpha\left(t\right)$ and $\beta\left(t\right)$ of the maximal distance $d\left(A\left(\alpha\left(t\right)\right),B\left(\beta\left(t\right)\right)\right)$, $t\in\left[0,1\right]$" [106, 107]. For convex contours, the Fréchet distance equals Hausdorff [7].

Sadeghi, Samiei, and Kittler investigated a variety of metrics, including the **Gradient Direction** (GD), for the fusion similarity measures in PCA and LDA. This metric "measures the distance between a query image and a gallery image in the gradient direction of the *a posteriori* probability function associated with the hypothesised client identity *k*" [2]. A combination of Gaussian distributions with isotropic covariance matrix is set as "density function representing the anti-class (world population) estimated from the data provided by other users $\left(\forall j\neq k\right)$. The diagonal elements of the isotropic covariance matrix are assumed to have values related to the magnitude of variation of the image data in the feature space". GD results to behave even more efficiently than the NC (normalised correlation) function. The matching score is defined as:

$$D_{GD}\left(x_i,x_{Ik}\right)=\frac{\left\|\left(x_i-x_{Ik}\right)^T\nabla_o P\left(k\mid x_i\right)\right\|}{\left\|\nabla_o P\left(k\mid x_i\right)\right\|}, \tag{9.10}$$

where, x_i is the test sample, x_I is the template of claimed identity, $\nabla_o P(k \mid x_i)$ represents the optimal gradient direction [2, 22].

Zhang and Wang proposed a faceprint technique. SIFT features are extrapolated from texture and range images, and matched. Fiducial points and **Geodesic Distance Ratios** (GDR) among models are adopted as matching scores, while **likelihood ratio**-based score level fusion is carried out to quantify the final score, *i.e.* a measure of similarity. Thanks to the robustness of SIFT, shape index, and geodesic distance against variations in geometric transformation, lighting, position, and emotion, the newly-developed faceprint approach is inherently non-sensitive to these changes. Given a set of fiducial points $\{x_{ik} \mid k = 1, ..., N\}$ on grid X^i, there is a collection of corresponding matching points $\{x_{jk} \mid k = 1, ..., N\}$ on grid X^j. The GDR(X^i, X^j) between X^i and X^j is defined as

$$D_{GDR}\left(X^i, X^j\right) = \frac{1}{N(N-1)/2} \sum_{k=1}^{N-1} \sum_{r=k+1}^{N} \frac{\min\left(gd\left(x_{ik}, x_{ir}\right), gd\left(x_{jk}, x_{jr}\right)\right)}{\max\left(gd\left(x_{ik}, x_{ir}\right), gd\left(x_{jk}, x_{jr}\right)\right)} \quad (9.11)$$

where, $gd(x_{ik}, x_{ir})$ is the geodesic distance between points x_{ik} and x_{ir}. According to its definition, GDR lies in the range $[0,1]$. The likelihood ratio-based fusion is formulated as below. Given a vector of K matching scores $s = [s_1, s_2, ..., s_K]$, and estimated genuine density $\hat{f}_{gen}(s)$ and impostor density $\hat{f}_{imp}(s)$, compute the likelihood ratio

$$LR(s) = \frac{\hat{f}_{gen}(s)}{\hat{f}_{imp}(s)}, \quad (9.12)$$

assign s to the genuine class if $LR(s) \geq \eta$. Zhang and Wang assumed the three matching scores to be independent between each other. Thus, the density function $\hat{f} = \prod_{k=1} \hat{f}_k(s_k)$ is adopted [158].

Saha and Bandyopadhyay proposed a new **line symmetry-based distance**. Its distance is given by the amount of line symmetry of a particular symmetrical line of cluster *i*. It is defined as:

$$D_{LS}(\bar{x}, i) = D_{SYM}(\bar{x}, \bar{p}_i) \times D_{Euclidean}(\bar{x}, \bar{c}), \quad (9.13)$$

where, $\bar{p}_i$ is the projected point on the relevant symmetrical line *i*, for a particular data point $\bar{x}$, $\bar{c}$ is the centroid of cluster *i*, *i.e.*, $\bar{c} = \left(\frac{m_{10}}{m_{00}}, \frac{m_{01}}{m_{00}} \right)$, and

$$D_{SYM}\left(\bar{x}, \bar{p}_i\right) = \frac{\sum_{i=1}^{knear} d_i}{knear}, \tag{9.14}$$

where, *knear* unique NN of $\bar{x}^* = 2 \times \bar{p}_i - \bar{x}$ are at Euclidean distances of $d_i s$, $i = 1, 2, ..., knear$ [159]. Lin, Peng, Xie, and Zheng proposed a new distance based on central symmetry to detect symmetrical patterns in datasets in face detection algorithms based on cluster analysis. Given *N* data objects $x_i, i = 1, 2, ..., N$, the distance between any pair of objects is defined as $D_{ij} = \left\| x_i - x_j \right\|$ and, given a centre vector $\vec{c}$, *e.g.* a cluster centroid, the distance between x_i and $\vec{c}$ is defined as $D_{ic} = \left\| x_i - \vec{c} \right\|$, which are two Minkowski distances. The **central symmetry distance** between a data object x_i and the centre vector $\vec{c}$ is

$$D_{central\_symmetry}\left(x_i, \vec{c}\right) = \left(\cos\alpha + k\right) \cdot \frac{\max\left(D_{ic}, D_{jc}\right)}{D_{ic} + D_{jc}}, \tag{9.15}$$

where, $i \neq j$ and α is the angle generated by vectors $\vec{D}_{ic} = x_i - \vec{c}$ and $\vec{D}_{jc} = x_j - \vec{c}$. The cosine of α can be computed according to the law of cosines:

$$\cos\alpha = \frac{D_{ic}^2 + D_{jc}^2 - D_{ij}^2}{2 D_{ic} D_{jc}}. \tag{9.16}$$

The variable *k* is such that $k \geq 2$. *k* is adopted "to adjust the result in different applications. When $D_{central\_symmetry}\left(x_i, \vec{c}\right)$ gets the minimum value, the object x_j is denoted as the symmetrical object relative to x_i with regard to the centroid $\vec{c}$" [160]. Su and Chou proposed a modification to *k*-means clustering algorithm for face detection. Similarly, the proposed algorithm adopts a new non-metric distance based on the idea of "point symmetry". Given *N* patterns, $x_i, i = 1, 2, ..., N$, and a reference vector $\vec{c}$, *e.g.*, a cluster centroid, the **point symmetry distance** between x_i and $\vec{c}$ is defined as

$$D_{PSD}\left(x_i, \vec{c}\right) = \min_{\substack{i=1,...,N \\ i \neq j}} \frac{\left\| \left(x_j - \vec{c}\right) + \left(x_i - \vec{c}\right) \right\|}{\left(\left\| x_j - \vec{c} \right\| + \left\| x_i - \vec{c} \right\| \right)}, \tag{9.17}$$

where, the denominator term is used as normalization in order to make the measure insensible to Euclidean distances $\|\cdot\|$ [161].

Hamdaoui and Tebbikh proposed the **weighted matrix distance** metric, relying on bi-dimensional matrices rather than on vectors and eigenvalues, for facial discrimination and verification. This measure quantifies the differences between two feature matrices obtained with bi-dimensional PCA and LDA (2DPCA and 2DLDA). "Each column of the feature matrix is multiplied by the inverse of the eigenvalue corresponding to the eigenvector of the projection matrix", as follows:

$$D_{WMD}\left(X_i, X_j\right) = \left(\sum_k \left(\frac{1}{\lambda_k} \sum_h \left(x_{ihk} - x_{jhk}\right)^2\right)^{p/2}\right)^{1/p}. \quad (9.18)$$

It coincides with the **Yang distance** for $p=1$ and with the **weighted Frobenius distance** for $p=2$. As a matter of fact, they also presented these two similarity measures for face recognition [25]. Turaga, Veeraraghavan, and Chellappa considered the two related Stiefel and Grassmann manifold, "which arise naturally in several vision applications such as spatiotemporal modelling, affine invariant shape analysis, image matching, and learning theory". In particular, they described tailored distances and parametric/non-parametric density estimators on these manifolds. These approaches are then adopted "to learn class conditional densities for applications in activity recognition, video-based face recognition, and shape classification". For comparison between shapes, they used the **arc-length distance** metric. It is given by the **Frobenius norm** of the angle between two subspaces [113].

Other measures were cited as possible similarity measures for face recognition: **Chamfer distance** [4, 92, 162], **reflection distance** [5], **template metric**, or **area of symmetric difference**, [5], **peak to sidelobe ratio** (PSR) [8], **cophenetic distance** [4], **Dice's coefficient** [163], **Bray Curtis** similarity measure [164], **Yambor distance** [74], **Matusita distance** [9]. For a deeper study on general similarity measures, namely not only for face recognition, the treatment is delayed to the work of Eidenberger, who evaluates similarity distances for content-based visual information retrieval. He divided the distance measures in two well-discriminated sets: "predicate-based (all vector elements are binary) and quantitative (all vector elements are continuous)". Particularly, he cited as other similarity measures of the first class: number of co-occurrencies, Russel and Rao, simple match coefficient, Kulczynski, Rogers and Tanimoto, Czekanovski, Sneath and Sokal, Hamann,

Ochiai, and Yule. Among the quantitative measures, he cited, in addition to the measures listed and contextualized above, Cohen, Catell, and Meehl index [165].

PERFORMANCES

Niennattrakul and Ratanamahatana evaluated the accuracy of **Euclidean distance**, **DTW**, and **histogram intersection distance** in a cluster algorithm for face image recognition. DTW outperforms Euclidean metric in all domains. Both these measures gave higher accuracy than HI distance [58].

Benedikt *et al.* conducted a literature review of pattern matching techniques applied to behavioural biometrics and evaluated the most distinguished techniques such as the **Fréchet distance**, **correlation coefficients**, **DTW**, **CDTW**, **DDTW**, and **Hidden Markov Models** (HMM). In addition, they proposed **Weighted hybrid derivative DTW** (WDTW). Performance comparisons showed that WDTW had the best recognition performance, followed by CDTW and DTW. The other measures had worse performances than these three [106, 107].

Chen tested an LBP-based face recognition algorithm under different similarity distances such as **taxicab**, **Euclidean**, **HI**, and the **weighted** version of HI (WHI). The results showed that the best performance was given by WHI [41].

Sadeghi, Samiei, and Kittler addressed the "problem of selecting and fusing similarity measures-based classifiers in LDA face space". **NC**, **correlation**, **GD**, **Euclidean**, **city block**, **Chebyshev** distances, χ^2 **statistic dissimilarity**, and **Canberra distance** were investigated. Results are achieved adopting the individual scoring function on both evaluation and test sets; manually positioned eyes locations are adopted for geometric normalization. Results clearly demonstrated that, among the individually-adopted metrics, the GD metric was "the outright winner". In a few cases, NC results were comparable to the one brought with the GD. The other distances gained worse performances. Results of a similar experiment with automatically-registered data show that even in this scenario the GD function "delivers a better or at least comparable performance" [2, 22].

Hamdaoui and Tebbikh compared face recognition accuracy with different distance metrics obtained changing parameter p in the **weighted matrix distance** for two-dimensional PCA and LDA. It coincides with the **Yang distance** for $p = 1$ and with the **weighted Frobenius distance** for $p = 2$. For all experiments, they varied the parameter p: $p = 0.125$, $p = 0.3$, $p = 0.5$, $p = 1$, and $p = 2$. The first tests are performed with 2D PCA algorithm. The Yang distance and the

Frobenius distances are less dependent on the number of eigenvectors compared to the others. However, fractional distances gave higher verification accuracy percentage with a lower number of eigenvectors. They concluded that "the recognition rate decreases as parameter p increases. The weighted Frobenius distance is the less efficient, but the weighted distance for $p = 0.125$ is the best one". As a matter of fact, the highest verification rate (95.50%) was achieved in conjunction with the adoption of the weighted distance metric ($p = 0.125$). The second set of experimentations was conducted adopting 2D LDA for feature extraction. Results showed the "superiority of the weighted AMD ($p = 0.125$) over the Yang ($p = 1$) and Frobenius ($p = 2$) distances for the first eigenvectors". They also compared 2D PCA and 2D LDA for extracting features and for facial verification. The plot clearly shows the accurate performances of the proposed weighted matrix distance metric over Frobenius, Yang, and standard AMD measures. The comparison accuracy given by PCA outperforms the accuracy obtained with LDA [25].

Table **6** summarized these performances.

Table 6: Features of other similarity measures

<table>
<tr><th>Similarity Measure</th><th>Metric</th><th>Algorithms</th><th>Face Data Type</th><th>Dimension</th><th>Reliability (Recognition Rate)</th><th>Sensitivity to Noise</th><th>Computational Cost</th><th>References</th></tr>
<tr><td rowspan="2">Dynamic Time Warping (DTW)</td><td rowspan="2">No</td><td>Clustering</td><td>Time Series Representation</td><td>2D</td><td>68.75%</td><td rowspan="7">Medium</td><td></td><td>Niennattrakul and Ratanamahatana in 2006 [58]</td></tr>
<tr><td rowspan="6">Matching</td><td rowspan="6">Point Cloud</td><td rowspan="6">3D</td><td rowspan="6">Quantified by a Graph</td><td>$O(mn)$: m and n are Lengths of Vectors</td><td rowspan="6">Benedikt and the Co-Authors in 2008 [106, 107]</td></tr>
<tr><td>Continuous DTW (CDTW)</td><td>No</td><td>Complexity Increases Combinatorially</td></tr>
<tr><td>Derivative DTW (DDTW)</td><td>No</td><td>$O(mn)$</td></tr>
<tr><td>Weighted Hybrid Derivative DTW (WDTW)</td><td>No</td><td>$O(mn)$</td></tr>
<tr><td>Fréchet Distance</td><td>yes</td><td>Medium</td></tr>
<tr><td>Hidden Markov Models</td><td></td><td>Medium</td></tr>
</table>

Similarity Measure	Metric	Algorithms	Face Data Type	Dimension	Reliability (Recognition Rate)	Sensitivity to Noise	Computational Cost	References
(HMM)								
Procrustes Distance	yes	NN for Face Image Recognition		2D	92.72%			Turaga, Veeraraghavan, and Chellappa in 2008 [113]
		Stiefel Procrustes Distance for Video Based Face Recognition			87.5%			
		Shape Procrustes Distance for Affine Shape Analysis			10%			
		Grassmann Manifold-Based Method			50%			
Arc-Length	Yes	Grassmann Manifold-Based Method			40%			
Histogram Intersection (HI)	No	Clustering	Time Series Representation	2D	62.94%			Niennattrakul and Ratanamahatana in 2006 [58]
		local binary pattern (LBP) method	LBP Histogram Sequences	2D	92%			Chen in 2008 [41]
Weighted Histogram Intersection (WHI)	No	local binary pattern (LBP) method	LBP Histogram Sequences	2D	93%		medium	
Yang Distance	Yes	2D PCA	Feature Matrices	2D	93%			Hamdaoui and Tebbikh in 2010 [25]
		2D Linear Discriminant Analysis (LDA)			93.5%			
Frobenius Distance	Yes	2D PCA			90%			
		2D LDA			92%			
Weighted AMD for *p=0.125*		2D PCA			95.5%			
		2D LDA			94%			
Gradient Direction	No	LDA		2D	TEE = 11.36; TET = 13.71			Sadeghi, Samiei, and Kittler [2, 22]
chi 2 Statistic Dissimilarity	Yes				TEE = 33.89; TET = 40.67			
Canberra Distance	Yes				TEE = 22.97; TET = 27.99			

CHAPTER 10

Discussion and Conclusion

Abstract: A thorough organized treatise of similarity measures for face recognition was presented. All these measures were applied to different typologies of recognition algorithms, so a direct and synoptic comparison of their performances is not possible. Nevertheless, many authors used many of these measures for their algorithms and compared the results, depending on the distances. These kinds of works are precious for making an evaluation and efficiency comparison of these measures, in order to give an overview on the way that can be used and employed for face recognition. This is the aim of the chapter. An analysis of requirements of face recognition algorithms is also provided for the applications of authentication and identification of suspects.

Keywords: Principal Component Analysis, Linear Discriminant Analysis, authentication, identification of suspects.

DISCUSSION

Mahalanobis distance seems to be the most accurate similarity measure for the most used recognition algorithms, namely the principal component analysis (PCA), or eigenface approach. But the most employed is surely the Euclidean distance, although its recognition rate is not as good as Mahalanobis and taxicab. Its best accuracy is associated with a PCA/LDA fusion algorithm. High rates are also given by cosine similarity measure and Tanimoto distance. Depending on the algorithm, a particular measure should be used. Chebyshev and Bhattacharyya distance were employed for their low computational cost, but Chebyshev recognition rates are not good enough to be taken into consideration.

Some measures do not have enough or adequate literature to allow a comparison and help developing a performance evaluation. For these measures, *i.e.* bottleneck, Procrustes, and earth mover's distance, recognition rates are not inserted in their chapters. Other measures, such as errors and similarity functions, are not properly suitable to a comparison, due to their definitions or their features. Likewise, their performances are not reported.

ANALYSIS

To help elaborating recognition algorithms, the features of algorithms and similarity measures are collected and correlated with some requirements necessary to *authentication*, for secure access to authorized personnel in strategic areas, and *identification* of suspects systems. Tables **7** and **8** show the requirements that these processes of authentication and identification, namely the most common face

Enrico Vezzetti and Federica Marcolin

recognition applications, must respect. The correlations between the requirements and the features of the similarity measure are valued with an exponential scale of 1 (low), 3 (medium), and 9 (high). These correlations describe the degree of necessity of a particular feature that a requirement has.

Table 7: Correlations between requirements and features of an authentication system. Connections are valued with an exponential scale of 1 (low), 3 (medium), and 9 (high). For instance, the value 1 between "metric" and "functionality in open spaces" means that in order to let the equipment connected to the authentication algorithm function in open spaces, a similarity measure that is not a metric may be used. In the second column, the importance of the requirement is specified with a scale between 1 and 5. Total absolute values and percentages of each feature are computed and reported in the last two lines

Authentication									
Requirement	**Importance of the Requirement [1 - 5]**	**Metric**	**Algorithm**	**Face Data Type**	**Dimension**	**Reliability**	**Sensitivity to Noise**	**Computational Cost**	
Functionality in Open Spaces	4	1	9	3	3	3	9	1	
Speed	5	3	9	9	3	3	3	9	
High Sensitivity (to Avoid Camouflages and Doubles)	5	3	9	3	9	9	9	1	
	Absolute Value	34	126	72	72	72	96	54	526
	Percentage	9	32	18	18	18	24	14	

Table 8: Correlations between requirements and features of an system for identification of suspects

Identification of Suspects									
Requirement	**Importance of the Requirement [1 - 5]**	**Metric**	**Algorithm**	**Face Data Type**	**Dimension**	**Reliability**	**Sensitivity to Noise**	**Computational Cost**	
Large Amounts of Data	5	1	9	9	3	1	3	9	
High Sensitivity (to Avoid Camouflages and Doubles)	5	3	9	1	3	9	9	1	
Ease of Interpretation	4	1	1	1	3	3	1	1	
	Absolute Value	24	94	54	42	62	64	54	394
	Percentage	6	24	14	11	16	16	14	

As expected, the type of algorithm, *i.e.* PCA, LDA, Gabor wavelets..., is an important feature for most of the requirements, while the fact that the similarity measure is a metric or not is almost contingent. Speed and high sensitivity are necessary requirements for an authentication system. Similarly, sensitivity, to void camouflages and doubles, is quite important also for identification.

CONCLUSION

A similarity measures treatise for face recognition was given. Every measure is defined and contextualized in face recognition field. Their applications in the state-of-the-art are presented and then summarized in a final table. These measures differ from each other for the algorithm they are used in, if they are metrics or not, the recognition rate, the computational cost, and the sensitivity to noise. It is quite inappropriate to provide general conclusions on their performances, but it is possible to summarize that the Euclidean, Manhattan, and especially Mahalanobis distances were often successfully applied to the most typical face recognition algorithm, namely principal component analysis (PCA). Another accurate distance is Bhattacharyya, whose computational cost in pairwise comparison-based algorithms was appreciated. Similarly, the Chebyshev distance was fairly employed for its low computational cost, although its performance recognition is not as good as the other Minkowski metrics. Generally, the new distance measures proposed by some authors are corrected and improved versions of common measures. Therefore, these novel measures generally gave better results than their respective predecessors. They are image Euclidean (IMED) distance for Euclidean, weighted hybrid derivative DTW (WDTW) for dynamic time warping (DTW), incremental Bhattacharyya distance (IBD) for Bhattacharyya, and doubly modified Hausdorff distance (M^2HD) for Hausdorff. Ever, the highest recognition rate was obtained with Euclidean distance when it is involved in a PCA/LDA fusion algorithm.

CHAPTER 11

Future Research

Abstract: This essential chapter is devoted to the hints of future research that this work has inspired. Embracing 3D is the main outcome of this brief analysis.

Keywords: 3D, landmark extraction, security, 3D ultrasound, 3D print.

FUTURE RESEARCH SPARKS

During the years working in the field, we have noticed that what is still missing in the framework of similarity measures for face recognition is the testing of these measures in the three-dimensional scenario of face recognition. The only distance which has been widely applied to 3D algorithms is Hausdorff distance, as can be seen from the table related to its performances.

The need of security in applications such as geographical borders and identification of subjects during bank transfer operations requires accurate methods and addresses research for this task. Furthermore, with the widespread usage of public video-based systems (CCTV) there are nowadays all the requirements for gaining more and more reliable security tools that could be responsive to this demand. The advantage of 3D approach is that it can guarantee this reliability. Facial landmark extraction [166-171] provides a univocal mapping of the face, independently of age and camouflages. This can be only partially gained through bi-dimensional tools.

Also, three-dimensional systems are currently a valuable option in the medical field, for instance by providing pediatricians and ultrasonographers with a more accurate prenatal diagnostic tool [172-175]. 3D ultrasound entirely shows foetuses' morphometry, supporting the practitioner in detecting diseases that could not be diagnosed through amniocentesis or blood tests. Moreover, 3D ultrasound represents a more comprehensive tool also for patients.

The new technology of 3D printing is also an advantage for those who are working on three-dimensional models.

Enrico Vezzetti and Federica Marcolin

A progress in the tools towards 3D has been successfully performed, but protocols of usage are still missing. Particularly, three-dimensional face recognition [176] has gained more and more attention for more than a decade. Similarity measures should be tested and employed also within this branch of the face recognition scenario.

REFERENCES

[1] K. Delac, M. Grgic, and P. Liatsis, "Appearance-based statistical methods for face recognition," *47th International Symposium ELMAR*, pp. 151-158, 2005.

[2] M. T. Sadeghi, M. Samiei, and J. Kittler, "Fusion of PCA-based and LDA-based similarity measures for face verification," *EURASIP Journal on Advances in Signal Processing*, p. 23, 2010.

[3] J. Yu, J. Amores, N. Sebe, P. Radeva, and Q. Tian, "Distance learning for similarity estimation," *Pattern Analysis and Machine Intelligence, IEEE Transactions on*, vol. 30, no. 3, pp. 451-462, 2008.

[4] T. Hertz, "Learning Distance Functions: Algo Rithms and Applications (Doctoral dissertation)," Jerusalem, 2006.

[5] A. P. D. K. Yüksek, "Hausdorff Distance for Shape Matching," İstanbul, 2010.

[6] T. Hlavaty, "3D object classification and retrieval," Pilsen, Czech Republic, 2003.

[7] R. C. Veltkamp, "Shape matching: Similarity measures and algorithms," *Shape Modeling and Applications, SMI 2001 International Conference on*, pp. 188-197, May 2001.

[8] R. S. Smith, "Angular Feature Extraction and EnsembleClassification Methods for 2D, 2.5 D and 3D FaceRecognition (Doctoral dissertation)," 2008.

[9] B. Huet, "Object Recognition from Large Libraries of Line Patterns (Doctoral dissertation)," 1999.

[10] B. A. Draper, W. S. Yambor, and J. R. Beveridge, "Analyzing pca-based face recognition algorithms: Eigenvector selection and distance measures," *Empirical Evaluation Methods in Computer Vision, Singapore*, pp. 1-15, 2002.

[11] J. Kittler, R. Ghaderi, T. Windeatt, and J. Matas, "Face Verification *via* ECOC," *BMVC*, pp. 1-10, September 2001.

[12] J. Kittler, R. Ghaderi, T. Windeatt, and J. Matas, "Face identification and verification *via* ECOC," *Audio-and Video-Based Biometric Person Authentication*, pp. 1-13, January 2001.

[13] J. Kittler, R. Ghaderi, T. Windeatt, and J. Matas, "Face verification *via* error correcting output codes," *Image and Vision Computing*, vol. 21, no. 13, pp. 1163-1169, 2003.

[14] C. Liu, "Gabor-based kernel PCA with fractional power polynomial models for face recognition," *Pattern Analysis and Machine Intelligence, IEEE Transactions on*, vol. 26, no. 5, pp. 572-581, 2004.

[15] C. Liu and H. Wechsler, "A Gabor feature classifier for face recognition," *Computer Vision. ICCV. Proceedings. Eighth IEEE International Conference on*, vol. 2, pp. 270-275, 2001.

[16] C. Liu and H. Wechsler, "Gabor feature based classification using the enhanced fisher linear discriminant model for face recognition," *Image processing, IEEE Transactions on*, vol. 11, no. 4, pp. 467-476, 2002.

[17] V. Perlibakas, "Distance measures for PCA-based face recognition," *Pattern Recognition Letters*, vol. 25, no. 6, pp. 711-724, 2004.

[18] Y. Zhao, "Learning user keystroke patterns for authentication," *Proceeding of World Academy of Science, Engineering and Technology*, vol. 14, pp. 65-70, December 2006.

[19] J. Park, Y. An, I. Jeong, G. Kang, and K. Pankoo, "Image indexing using spatial multi-resolution color correlogram," *Imaging Systems and Techniques. IST'07. IEEE International Workshop on*, pp. 1-4, May 2007.

[20] Y. Liu, D. Zhang, G. Lu, and W. Y. Ma, "A survey of content-based image retrieval with high-level semantics," *Pattern Recognition*, vol. 40, no. 1, pp. 262-282, 2007.

[21] R. S. Smith, J. Kittler, M. Hamouz, and J. Illingworth, "Face recognition using angular LDA and SVM ensembles," *Pattern Recognition. ICPR. 18th International Conference on*, vol. 3, pp. 1008-1012, August 2006.

[22] M. T. Sadeghi, M. Samiei, and J. Kittler, "Selection and fusion of similarity measure based classifiers using support vector machines," *Structural, Syntactic, and Statistical Pattern Recognition*, pp. 479-488, 2008.

[23] D. Omaia and L. V. Batista, "2D-DCT distance based face recognition using a reduced number of coefficients," *Computer Graphics and Image Processing (SIBGRAPI), XXII Brazilian Symposium on*, pp. 291-298, October 2009.

[24] Z. Cai, F. L. Wang, and A. H. Xu, "A new image distance for KFDA," *Image and Signal Processing (CISP), 3rd International Congress on*, vol. 4, pp. 1740-1744, October 2010.

[25] C. Rouabhia, K. Hamdaoui, and H. Tebbikh, "Weighted matrix distance metric for face images classification," *Machine and Web Intelligence (ICMWI), International Conference on*, pp. 312-316, October 2010.

[26] W. Yan, Q. Liu, H. Lu, and S. Ma, "Dynamic similarity kernel for visual recognition," *Knowledge-Based Intelligent Information and Engineering Systems*, pp. 47-54, January 2006.

[27] M. Artiklar, M. Hassoun, and P. Watta, "Application of a postprocessing algorithm for improved human face recognition," *Proceedings of the IEEE International Conference on Neural Networks*, pp. 10-16, 1999.

[28] A. J. O'Toole, Y. Cheng, P. J. Phillips, B. Ross, and H. A. Wild, "Face recognition algorithms as models of human face processing," *Automatic Face and Gesture Recognition. Proceedings. Fourth IEEE International Conference on*, pp. 552-557, 2000.

[29] J. R. Beveridge, K. She, B. Draper, and G. H. Givens, "Parametric and nonparametric methods for the statistical evaluation of human id algorithms," *Proc. 3rd Workshop on the Empirical Evaluation of Computer Vision Systems*, December 2001.

[30] F. Jiao, W. Gao, X. Chen, G. Cui, and S. Shan, "A face recognition method based on local feature analysis," *Proc. of the 5th Asian Conference on Computer Vision*, pp. 188-192, January 2002.

[31] H. Ebrahimpour-Komleh, "Fractal techniques for face recognition," Queensland University of Technology, 2006.

[32] H. Ebrahimpour and A. Kouzani, "Face Recognition Using Bagging KNN," Queensland University of Technology,.

[33] T. Arodź, "New Radon-Based Translation, Rotation, and Scaling Invariant Transform for Face Recognition," *Computational Science-ICCS*, pp. 9-17, 2004.

[34] J. Yang, X. Gao, D. Zhang, and J. Y. Yang, "Kernel ICA: An alternative formulation and its application to face recognition," *Pattern Recognition*, vol. 38, no. 10, pp. 1784-1787, 2005.

[35] K. Delac, M. Grgic, and S. Grgic, "Face recognition in JPEG and JPEG2000 compressed domain," *Image and Vision Computing*, vol. 27, no. 8, pp. 1108-1120, 2009.

[36] F. Matta and J. L. Dugelay, "Person recognition using human head motion information," *Articulated motion and deformable objects*, pp. 326-335, 2006.

[37] J. Shi, A. Samal, and D. Marx, "How effective are landmarks and their geometry for face recognition?," *Computer Vision and Image Understanding*, vol. 102, no. 2, pp. 117-133, 2006.

[38] R. V. Yampolskiy and V. Govindaraju, "Similarity measure functions for strategy-based biometrics," *International Conference on Signal Processing*, pp. 174-179, October 2006.

[39] R. V. Yampolskiy and V. Govindaraju, "Behavioural biometrics: a survey and classification," *International Journal of Biometrics*, vol. 1, no. 1, pp. 81-113, 2008.

[40] K. E. Graves and R. Nagarajah, "Uncertainty estimation using fuzzy measures for multiclass classification," *Neural Networks, IEEE Transactions on*, vol. 18, no. 1, pp. 128-140, 2007.

[41] C. Chen, "Decision level fusion of hybrid local features for face recognition," *Neural Networks and Signal Processing, International Conference on*, pp. 199-204, June 2008.

[42] S. A. Dawwd and B. S. Mahmood, "A reconfigurable interconnected filter for face recognition based on convolution neural network," *Design and Test Workshop (IDT), 4th International*, pp. 1-6, November 2009.

[43] M. Orozco-Alzate and C. G. Castellanos-Domínguez, "Trends in Nearest Feature Classification for Face Recognition—Achievements and Perspectives," in *State of the Art in Face Recognition*. Vienna, Austria: I-Tech, 2009, pp. 978-3.

[44] A. Izmailov and A. Krzyżak, "On Improving the Efficiency of Eigenface Using a Novel Facial Feature Localization," *Image Analysis and Processing–ICIAP*, pp. 414-424, 2009.

[45] M. A. Turk and A. P. Pentland, "Face recognition using eigenfaces," *Computer Vision and Pattern Recognition. Proceedings CVPR'91., IEEE Computer Society Conference on*, pp. 586-591, June 1991.

[46] G. G. Gordon, "Face recognition based on depth and curvature features," *Computer Vision and Pattern Recognition. Proceedings CVPR'92., IEEE Computer Society Conference on*, pp. 808-810, June 1992.

[47] Z. Lipoščak and S. Loncaric, "A scale-space approach to face recognition from profiles," *Computer Analysis of Images and Patterns*, pp. 243-250, January 1999.

[48] A. B. Moreno, A. Sánchez, J. F. Vélez, and F. J. Díaz, "Face recognition using 3D surface-extracted descriptors," *Irish Machine Vision and Image Processing Conference*, vol. 2, September 2003.

[49] C. Xu, Y. Wang, T. Tan, and L. Quan, "Automatic 3D face recognition combining global geometric features with local shape variation information," *Automatic face and gesture recognition. Proceedings. Sixth IEEE international conference on*, pp. 308-313, May 2004.

[50] O. Arandjelović and R. Cipolla, "Face recognition from face motion manifolds using robust kernel resistor-average distance," *Computer Vision and Pattern Recognition Workshop CVPRW'04. IEEE Conference on*, pp. 88-88, 2004.

[51] O. Arandjelović and R. Cipolla, "A pose-wise linear illumination manifold model for face recognition using video," *Computer vision and image understanding*, vol. 113, no. 1, pp. 113-125, 2009.

[52] Y. Lee, H. Song, U. Yang, H. Shin, and K. Sohn, "Local feature based 3D face recognition," *Audio- and Video-Based Biometric Person Authentication*, pp. 909-918, January 2005.

[53] M. Hüsken, M. Brauckmann, S. Gehlen, and C. Von der Malsburg, "Strategies and benefits of fusion of 2D and 3D face recognition," *Computer Vision and Pattern Recognition-Workshops. CVPR Workshops. IEEE Computer Society Conference on*, pp. 174-174, June 2005.

[54] L. Wang, Y. Zhang, and J. Feng, "On the Euclidean distance of images," *Pattern Analysis and Machine Intelligence, IEEE Transactions on*, vol. 27, no. 8, pp. 1334-1339, 2005.

[55] A. M. Bronstein, M. M. Bronstein, and R. Kimmel, "Expression-invariant face recognition *via* spherical embedding," *Image Processing. IEEE International Conference on*, vol. 3, pp. III-756, September 2005.

[56] A. M. Bronstein, M. M. Bronstein, and R. Kimmel, "Robust expression-invariant face recognition from partially missing data," *Computer Vision–ECCV*, pp. 396-408, 2006.

[57] R. S. Senaratne and S. K. Halgamuge, "Optimal weighting of landmarks for face recognition," *Journal of Multimedia*, vol. 1, no. 3, pp. 31-41, 2006.

[58] V. Niennattrakul and C. A. Ratanamahatana, "Clustering multimedia data using time series," *Hybrid Information Technology. ICHIT'06. International Conference on*, vol. 1, pp. 372-379, November 2006.

[59] S. Gupta, J. K. Aggarwal, M. K. Markey, and A. C. Bovik, "3D face recognition founded on the structural diversity of human faces," *Computer Vision and Pattern Recognition. CVPR'07. IEEE Conference on*, pp. 1-7, June 2007.

[60] Y. Gizatdinova and V. Surakka, "Automatic localization of facial landmarks from expressive images of high complexity," 2008.

[61] F. Tunçer, "3D Face Representation and Recognition Using Spherical Harmonics (PhD Dissertation)," 2008.

[62] B. Klare, P. Mallapragada, A. K. Jain, and K. Davis, "Clustering face carvings: Exploring the devatas of Angkor Wat," *Pattern Recognition (ICPR), 20th International Conference on*, pp. 1517-1520, August 2010.

[63] D. B. Ober, S. P. Neugebauer, and P. A. Sallee, "Training and feature-reduction techniques for human identification using anthropometry," *Biometrics: Theory Applications and Systems (BTAS), Fourth IEEE International Conference on*, pp. 1-8, September 2010.

[64] Y., Zhu, Q., Chen, Y., and Pan, J. S. Xu, "An improvement to the nearest neighbor classifier and face recognition experiments," *Int J Innov Comput Inf Control*, vol. 8, no. 12, pp. 1349-4198, 2012.

[65] C., Liu, C., Wu, N., Wu, X., Li, Y., and Wang, Z. Yang, "Collaborative representation with reduced residual for face recognition," *Neural Computing and Applications*, vol. 25, no. 7-8, pp. 1741-1754, 2014.

[66] D. M. J. Tax, R. Duin, and D. De Ridder, *Classification, Parameter Estimation and State Estimation: An Engineering Approach Using MATLAB.*: John Wiley and Sons, 2004.

[67] M. Trias, "Face verification based on Support Vector Machine (PhD dissertation)," Lausanne, 2005.

[68] D. Cohen-Steiner, H. Edelsbrunner, and J. Harer, "Stability of persistence diagrams," *Discrete & Computational Geometry*, vol. 37, no. 1, pp. 103-120, 2007.

[69] T. Sim, R. Sukthankar, M. Mullin, and S. Baluja, "Memory-based face recognition for visitor identification," *Automatic Face and Gesture Recognition. Proceedings. Fourth IEEE International Conference on*, pp. 214-220, 2000.

[70] S. Yilmaz and M. Artiklar, "On Recognizing Human Faces from Frontal Views," *KSU Journal of Science and Engineering*, vol. 8, no. 1, pp. 41-44, 2005.
[71] K. I. Chang, K. W. Bowyer, and P. J. Flynn, "An evaluation of multimodal 2D+ 3D face biometrics," *Pattern Analysis and Machine Intelligence, IEEE Transactions on*, vol. 27, no. 4, pp. 619-624, 2005.
[72] A. Yao, G. Wang, X. Lin, and X. Chai, "An incremental Bhattacharyya dissimilarity measure for particle filtering," *Pattern Recognition*, vol. 43, no. 4, pp 1244-1256, 2010.
[73] V. Zoonekynd, "http://zoonek2.free.fr/UNIX/," consulted on 21/10/2014.
[74] S. Katadound, "Face Recognition: Study and Comparison of PCA and EBGM Algorithms (Master of Science Degree Thesis)," 2004.
[75] J. Shi, A. Samal, and D. Marx, "Face recognition using landmark-based bidimensional regression," *Data Mining, Fifth IEEE International Conference on*, p. 4, November 2005.
[76] K. Seshadri and M. Savvides, "Robust modified active shape model for automatic facial landmark annotation of frontal faces," *Biometrics: Theory, Applications, and Systems. BTAS'09. IEEE 3rd International Conference on*, pp. 1-8, September 2009.
[77] R. Abiantun, U. Prabhu, K. Seshandri, J. Heo, and M. Savvides, "An Analysis of Facial Shape and Texture for Recognition: A Large Scale Evaluation on FRGC ver2.0," *IEEE Workshop on Applications of Computer Vision*, pp. 212-219, 2011.
[78] C. S. McCool, "Hybrid 2D and 3D face verification (PhD Dissertation)," 2007.
[79] B. Amberg, R. Knothe, and T. Vetter, "Expression invariant 3D face recognition with a morphable model. In Automatic Face & Gesture Recognition," *FG'08. 8th IEEE International Conference on*, pp. 1-6, 2008.
[80] B. Moghaddam and A. Pentland, "Probabilistic visual learning for object representation," *Pattern Analysis and Machine Intelligence, IEEE Transactions on*, vol. 19, no. 7, pp. 696-710, 1997.
[81] K. K. Sung and T. Poggio, "Example-based learning for view-based human face detection," *Pattern Analysis and Machine Intelligence, IEEE Transactions on*, vol. 20, no. 1, pp. 39-51, 1998.
[82] D. G. Sim, O. K. Kwon, and R. H. Park, "Object matching algorithms using robust Hausdorff distance measures," *IEEE Transactions on Image Processing*, vol. 8, no. 3, pp. 425-429, 1999.
[83] M. P. Dubuisson and A. K. Jain, "A modified Hausdorff distance for object matching. In Pattern Recognition, 1994. Vol. 1-Conference A: Computer Vision & Image Processing," *Proceedings of the 12th IAPR International Conference on,* vol. 1, pp. 566-568, October 1994.
[84] B. Achermann and H. Bunke, "Classifying Range Images of Human Faces with Hausdorff Distance," *Pattern Recognition, 15th IEEE International Conference on*, vol. 2, pp. 809-813, 2000.
[85] D. P. Huttenlocher, G. A. Klanderman, and W. J. Rucklidge, "Comparing images using the Hausdorff distance," *Pattern Analysis and Machine Intelligence, IEEE Transactions on*, vol. 15, no. 9, pp. 850-863, 1993.
[86] C. F. Olson and D. P. Huttenlocher, "Recognition by matching dense, oriented edge pixels," *Computer Vision. Proceedings., International Symposium on*, pp. 91-96, November 1995.
[87] B. Takács, "Comparing face images using the modified Hausdorff distance," *Pattern Recognition*, vol. 31, no. 12, pp. 1873-1881, 1998.
[88] O. Jesorsky, K. J. Kirchberg, and R. W. Frischholz, "Robust face detection using the hausdorff distance," *Audio-and video-based biometric person authentication*, pp. 90-95, January 2001.
[89] Y. Gao and M. K. Leung, "Line segment Hausdorff distance on face matching," *Pattern Recognition*, vol. 35, no. 2, pp. 361-371, 2002.
[90] Y. Gao, "Efficiently comparing face images using a modified Hausdorff distance," *IEE Proceedings-Vision, Image and Signal Processing*, vol. 150, no. 6, pp. 346-350, 2003.
[91] Y. H. Lee and J. C. Shim, "Curvature based human face recognition using depth weighted hausdorff distance," *Image Processing. ICIP'04. International Conference on*, vol. 3, pp. 1429-1432, October 2004.
[92] E. Baudrier, G. Millon, F. Nicolier, and S. Ruan, "The adaptative local hausdorff-distance map as a new dissimilarity measure," *Pattern Recognition*, vol. 41, pp. 1461-1478, 2004.
[93] É. Baudrier, F. Nicolier, G. Millon, and S. Ruan, "Binary-image comparison with local-dissimilarity quantification," *Pattern Recognition*, vol. 41, no. 5, pp. 1461-1478, 2008.
[94] T. D. Russ, M. W. Koch, and C. Q. Little, "A 2D range Hausdorff approach for 3D face recognition," *Computer Vision and Pattern Recognition-Workshops. CVPR Workshops. IEEE Computer Society Conference on*, pp. 169-169, June 2005.

[95] I. A. Kakadiaris, H. Abdelmunim, W. Yang, and T. Theoharis, "Profile-based face recognition," *Automatic Face & Gesture Recognition. FG'08. 8th IEEE International Conference on*, pp. 1-8, September 2008.

[96] B. Efraty, E. Bilgazyev, S. Shah, and I. A. Kakadiaris, "Profile-based 3D-aided face recognition," *Pattern Recognition*, vol. 45, no. 1, pp. 43-53, 2012.

[97] T. Gevers and A. W. M. Smeulders, "Image search engines: An overview," *Emerging Topics in Computer Vision*, pp. 1-54, 2004.

[98] H. Wu, Y. Yoshida, and T. Shioyama, "Optimal Gabor filters for high speed face identification," *Pattern Recognition, 2002. Proceedings. 16th International Conference on*, vol. 1, pp. 107-110, 2002.

[99] W. Zhang, S. Shan, H. Zhang, W. Gao, and X. Chen, "Multi-resolution histograms of local variation patterns (MHLVP) for robust face recognition," *Audio-and Video-Based Biometric Person Authentication*, pp. 937-944, January 2005.

[100] V. Perlibakas, "Face recognition using principal component analysis and log-gabor filters," *arXiv preprint cs/0605025*, 2005.

[101] M. C. Ionita, "Advances in the design of statistical face modelling techniques for face recognition (Doctoral dissertation)," Galway, 2008.

[102] M. T. Ibrahim, L. Guan, and M. K. K. Niazi, "Horizontal features based illumination normalization method for face recognition," *7th International Symposium on Image and Signal Processing and Analysis*, pp. 684-689, September 2011.

[103] N. C. Kim, Y. A. Ju, H. J. So, and M. H. Kim, "Face recognition using multi-lag directional local correlations," *IEEE International Conference on Multimedia and Expo*, pp. 1-6, July 2011.

[104] A. Li, S. Shan, X. Chen, and W. Gao, "Face recognition based on non-corresponding region matching," *IEEE International Conference on Computer Vision*, pp. 1060-1067, November 2011.

[105] W. S. Chu, J. C. Chen, and J. J. J. Lien, "Kernel discriminant transformation for image set-based face recognition," *Pattern Recognition*, vol. 44, no. 8, pp. 1567-1580, 2011.

[106] L. Benedikt, D. Cosker, P. L. Rosin, and D. Marshall, "3D facial gestures in biometrics: from feasibility study to application," *Biometrics: Theory, Applications and Systems BTAS. 2nd IEEE International Conference on*, pp. 1-6, 2008.

[107] L. Benedikt, V. Kajic, D. Cosker, P. L. Rosin, and A. D. Marshall, "Facial Dynamics in Biometric Identification," *BMVC*, pp. 1-10, 2008.

[108] F. Chazal, D. Cohen-Steiner, L. J. Guibas, F. Mémoli, and S. Y. Oudot, "Gromov-Hausdorff Stable Signatures for Shapes using Persistence," *Computer Graphics Forum*, vol. 28, no. 5, pp. 1393-1403, July 2009.

[109] I. L. Dryden and K. V. Mardia, *Statistical shape analysis (Vol. 4)*. New York: John Wiley & Sons, 1998.

[110] I. L. Dryden, "Statistical Shape Analysis in High-Level Vision," *IMA Volumes in Mathematics and its Applications*, vol. 133, pp. 37-56, 2003.

[111] L. H. Clemmensen, D. D. Gomez, and B. K. Ersbøll, "Individual discriminative face recognition models based on subsets of features," *Image Analysis*, pp. 61-71, 2007.

[112] R. Chellappa, M. Bicego, and P. Turaga, "Video-Based Face Recognition Algorithms," *Handbook of Remote Biometrics, Advances in Pattern Recognition*, pp. 193-216, 2009.

[113] P. Turaga, A. Veeraraghavan, and R. Chellappa, "Statistical analysis on Stiefel and Grassmann manifolds with applications in computer vision," *Computer Vision and Pattern Recognition. CVPR. IEEE Conference on*, pp. 1-8, June 2008.

[114] P. Perakis, T. Theoharis, G. Passalis, and I. A. Kakadiaris, "Automatic 3D Facial Region Retrieval from Multi-pose Facial Datasets," *3DOR*, pp. 37-44, March 2009.

[115] H. M. Rara *et al.*, "Distant face recognition based on sparse-stereo reconstruction," *Image Processing (ICIP) 16th IEEE International Conference on*, pp. 4141-4144, November 2009.

[116] H. Rara *et al.*, "A framework for long distance face recognition using dense-and sparse-stereo reconstruction," *Advances in Visual Computing*, pp. 774-783, 2009.

[117] H. Rara *et al.*, "Face recognition at-a-distance based on sparse-stereo reconstruction," *Computer Vision and Pattern Recognition Workshops. CVPR Workshops. IEEE Computer Society Conference on*, pp. 27-32, June 2009.

[118] W. Surong, C. Liang-Tien, and D. Rajan, "Efficient image retrieval using MPEG-7 descriptors," *Image Processing. ICIP. Proceedings. International Conference on*, vol. 3, pp. III-509, September 2003.

[119] W. Surong, C. Liang-Tien, and D. Rajan, "Image Retrieval Using Dominant Color Descriptor," Singapore, 2008.

[120] J. Li, Y. Wang, and T. Tan, "Video-based face recognition using earth mover's distance," *Audio-and Video-Based Biometric Person Authentication*, pp. 229-238, January 2005.

[121] D. Xu, S. Yan, and J. Luo, "Face recognition using spatially constrained earth mover's distance," *Image Processing, IEEE Transactions on*, vol. 17, no. 11, pp. 2256-2260, 2008.

[122] W. Zhou, A. Ahrary, and S. I. Kamata, "Face Recognition using Local Quaternion Patters and Weighted Spatially constrained Earth Mover's Distance," *Consumer Electronics. ISCE'09. IEEE 13th International Symposium on*, pp. 285-289, May 2009.

[123] T. Sim and S. Zhang, "Exploring Face Space," *Computer Vision and Pattern Recognition Workshop. CVPRW '04. Conference on*, p. 84, June 2004.

[124] A. S. Manikarnika, "A General Face Recognition System (Master of Science Degree Thesis)," 2006.

[125] K. Bernardin, R. Stiefelhagen, and A. Waibel, "Probabilistic integration of sparse audio-visual cues for identity tracking," *Proceedings of the 16th ACM international conference on Multimedia*, pp. 151-158, 2008.

[126] I. Paliy, A. Sachenko, Y. Kurylyak, O. Boumbarov, and S. Sokolov, "Combined approach to face detection for biometric identification systems," *Intelligent Data Acquisition and Advanced Computing Systems: Technology and Applications. IDAACS. IEEE International Workshop on*, pp. 425-429, September 2009.

[127] D. Cristinacce, T. F. Cootes, and I. M. Scott, "A Multi-Stage Approach to Facial Feature Detection," *BMVC*, pp. 1-10, 2004.

[128] D. Cristinacce and T. F. Cootes, "Feature Detection and Tracking with Constrained Local Models," *BMVC*, vol. 2, no. 5, p. 6, September 2006.

[129] D. Cristinacce and T. F. Cootes, "Boosted Regression Active Shape Models," *BMVC*, pp. 1-10, September 2007.

[130] G. M. Beumer, Q. Tao, A. M. Bazen, and R. N. Veldhuis, "A landmark paper in face recognition. In Automatic Face and Gesture Recognition," *FGR. 7th International Conference on*, pp. 6 pp.-78, 2006.

[131] M. Lades *et al.*, "Distortion invariant object recognition in the dynamic link architecture," *Computers, IEEE Transactions on*, vol. 42, no. 3, pp. 300-311, 1993.

[132] L. Wiskott, "Phantom faces for face analysis," *Computer Analysis of Images and Patterns*, pp. 480-487, January 1997.

[133] L. Wiskott, J. M. Fellous, N. Kuiger, and C. Von Der Malsburg, "Face recognition by elastic bunch graph matching," *Pattern Analysis and Machine Intelligence, IEEE Transactions on*, vol. 19, no. 7, pp. 775-779, 1997.

[134] L. Wiskott, "The role of topographical constraints in face recognition," *Pattern Recognition Letters*, vol. 20, no. 1, pp. 89-96, 1999.

[135] K. C. Chung, S. C. Kee, and S. R. Kim, "Face recognition using principal component analysis of Gabor filter responses," *Recognition, Analysis, and Tracking of Faces and Gestures in Real-Time Systems, Proceedings. International Workshop on*, pp. 53-57, 1999.

[136] B. Duc, S. Fischer, and J. Bigun, "Face authentication with Gabor information on deformable graphs," *Image Processing, IEEE Transactions on*, vol. 8, no. 4, pp. 504-516, 1999.

[137] R. Liao and S. Z. Li, "Face recognition based on multiple facial features," *Automatic Face and Gesture Recognition. Proceedings. Fourth IEEE International Conference on*, pp. 239-244, 2000.

[138] Y. Wang, C. S. Chua, and Y. K. Ho, "Facial feature detection and face recognition from 2D and 3D images," *Pattern Recognition Letters*, vol. 23, no. 10, pp. 1191-1202, 2002.

[139] M. J. Escobar and J. Ruiz-del-Solar, "Biologically-based face recognition using Gabor filters and log-polar images," *Proceedings of the International Joint Conference on Neural Networks*, vol. 2, pp. 1143-1147, 2002.

[140] B. Kepenekci, F. Boray Tek, and G. B. Akar, "Occluded face recognition based on Gabor wavelets," *Image Processing. Proceedings. International Conference on*, vol. 1, pp. I-293, 2002.

[141] A. Pentland, B. Moghaddam, and T. Starner, "View-based and modular eigenspaces for face recognition," *Computer Vision and Pattern Recognition. Proceedings CVPR'94., IEEE Computer Society Conference on*, pp. 84-91, June 1994.

[142] B. Moghaddam and A. Pentland, "Probabilistic visual learning for object detection," *Computer Vision. Proceedings., Fifth International Conference on*, pp. 786-793, June 1995.

[143] B. Moghaddam, C. Nastar, and A. Pentland, "A Bayesian similarity measure for direct image matching," *Pattern Recognition, 1996., Proceedings of the 13th International Conference on*, vol. 2, pp. 350-358, August 1996.

[144] B. Moghaddam, W. Wahid, and A. Pentland, "Beyond eigenfaces: Probabilistic matching for face recognition," *Automatic Face and Gesture Recognition. Proceedings. Third IEEE International Conference on*, pp. 30-35, April 1998.

[145] B. Moghaddam, T. Jebara, and A. Pentland, "Bayesian face recognition," *Pattern Recognition*, vol. 33, no. 11, pp. 1771-1782, 2000.

[146] L. Zhang, L. Chen, M. Li, and H. Zhang, "Automated annotation of human faces in family albums," *Proceedings of the eleventh ACM international conference on Multimedia*, pp. 355-358, November 2003.

[147] X. Wang and X. Tang, "Bayesian face recognition using Gabor features," *Proceedings of the 2003 ACM SIGMM workshop on Biometrics methods and applications*, pp. 70-73, November 2003.

[148] S. Santini and R. Jain, "Similarity queries in image databases," *Computer Vision and Pattern Recognition Proceedings CVPR'96, IEEE Computer Society Conference on*, pp. 646-651, June 1996.

[149] S. Santini and R. Jain, "Similarity measures," *Pattern analysis and machine intelligence, IEEE transactions on*, vol. 21, no. 9, pp. 871-883, 1999.

[150] M. R., Solihah, B. Widyanto, "A New Face Shape Representation Method for Facial Identification Software: A Study of IT Application for Police Department, Republic of Indonesia," Trisak, Republic of Indonesia,.

[151] A. B. Hamza and H. Krim, "Geodesic matching of triangulated surfaces," *Image Processing, IEEE Transactions on*, vol. 15, no. 8, pp. 2249-2258, 2006.

[152] M. Oussalah, "Content based image retrieval: review of state of art and future directions," *Image Processing Theory, Tools and Applications. IPTA 2008. First Workshops on*, pp. 1-10, November 2008.

[153] T. Ahonen, A. Hadid, and M. Pietikäinen, "Face recognition with local binary patterns," *Computer vision-eccv*, pp. 469-481, 2004.

[154] Z. Yue and R. Chellappa, "Pose-normalized View Synthesis from Silhouettes," *IEEE International Conference on Acoustics, Speech, and Signal Processing*, pp. 569-572, 2005.

[155] Z. Yue and R. Chellappa, "Synthesis of silhouettes and visual hull reconstruction for articulated humans," *Multimedia, IEEE Transactions on*, vol. 10, no. 8, pp. 1565-1577, 2008.

[156] B. Kim and J. P. Yoon, "Similarity measurement for aggregation of spatial objects," *Proceedings of the 2005 ACM symposium on Applied computing*, pp. 1213-1217, March 2005.

[157] V. Niennattrakul, D. Wanichsan, and C. A. Ratanamahatana, "Hand geometry verification using time series representation," *Knowledge-Based Intelligent Information and Engineering Systems*, pp. 824-831, January 2007.

[158] G. Zhang and Y. Wang, "Faceprint: fusion of local features for 3D face recognition," *Advances in biometrics*, pp. 394-403, 2009.

[159] S. Saha and S. Bandyopadhyay, "A new line symmetry distance and its application to data clustering," *Journal of Computer Science and Technology*, vol. 24, no. 3, pp. 544-556, 2009.

[160] J. Y. Lin, H. Peng, J. M. Xie, and Q. L. Zheng, "Novel clustering algorithm based on central symmetry," *Machine Learning and Cybernetics, 2004. Proceedings of 2004 International Conference on*, vol. 3, pp. 1329-1334, August 2004.

[161] M. C. Su and C. H. Chou, "A modified version of the K-means algorithm with a distance based on cluster symmetry," *IEEE Transactions on pattern analysis and machine intelligence*, vol. 23, no. 6, pp. 674-680, 2001.

[162] S. Loncaric, "A survey of shape analysis techniques," *Pattern recognition*, vol. 31, no. 8, pp. 983-1001, 1998.

[163] B. Zaka, "Theory and Applications of Similarity Detection Techniques (Doctoral dissertation)," 2009.

[164] J. A. Montoya Zegarra, N. J. Leite, and R. da Silva Torres, "Wavelet-based fingerprint image retrieval," *Journal of computational and applied mathematics*, vol. 227, no. 2, pp. 294-307, 2009.

[165] H. Eidenberger, "Evaluation and analysis of similarity measures for content-based visual information retrieval," *Multimedia systems*, vol. 12, no. 2, pp. 71-87, 2006.

[166] E. Vezzetti and Marcolin F., "Geometrical descriptors for human face morphological analysis and recognition," *Robotics and Autonomous Systems*, vol. 60, no. 6, pp. 928-939, 2012.

[167] E. Vezzetti and Marcolin F., "Geometry-based 3D face morphology analysis: soft-tissue landmark formalization," *Multimedia Tools and Applications*, pp. 1-35, 2012.

[168] E. Vezzetti and Marcolin F., "3D human face description: landmarks measures and geometrical features," *Image and Vision Computing*, vol. 30, no. 10, pp. 698-712, 2012.

[169] E. Vezzetti and F. Marcolin, "3D Landmarking in Multiexpression Face Analysis: A Preliminary Study on Eyebrows and Mouth," *Aesthetic Plastic Surgery*, vol. 38, pp. 796–811, 2014.

[170] E. Vezzetti, F. Marcolin, and V. Stola, "3D Human Face Soft Tissues Landmarking Method: An Advanced Approach," *Computers in Industry*, vol. 64, no. 9, pp. 1326–1354, 2013.

[171] E. Vezzetti, S. Moos, F. Marcolin, and V. Stola, "A pose-independent method for 3D face landmark formalization," *Computer Methods and Programs in Biomedicine*, vol. 198, no. 3, pp. 1078-1096, 2012.

[172] F. Calignano and E. Vezzetti, "Soft tissue diagnosis in maxillofacial surgery: a preliminary study on three-dimensional face geometrical features-based analysis," *Aesthetic plastic surgery*, vol. 34, no. 2, pp. 200-211, 2010.

[173] E. Vezzetti, F. Calignano, and S. Moos, "Computer-aided morphological analysis for maxillo-facial diagnostic: a preliminary study," *Journal of Plastic, Reconstructive & Aesthetic Surgery*, vol. 63, no. 2, pp. 218-226, 2010.

[174] E. Vezzetti, D. Speranza, F. Marcolin, and G. Fracastoro, "Exploiting 3D Ultrasound for Fetal Diagnosis Purpose through Facial Landmarking," *Image Analysis & Stereology*, vol. 33, no. 3, pp. 167-188, 2014.

[175] S. Moos *et al.*, "Cleft lip pathology diagnosis and foetal landmark extraction *via* 3D geometrical analysis," *International Journal on Interactive Design and Manufacturing*, pp. 1-18, 2014.

[176] E. Vezzetti, F. Marcolin, and G. Fracastoro, "3D face recognition: An automatic strategy based on geometrical descriptors and landmarks," *Robotics and Autonomous Systems*, vol. 62, no. 12, pp. 1768-1776, 2014.

Subject Index

I

J

K

L

M

N

O

P

Made in United States
Orlando, FL
05 November 2026

90219448R00069